LEAD
YOURSELF
TO SUCCESS

YOUR GUIDE TO PROSPERITY

PIERRE ST. JEAN, ESQUIRE

Attorney at Law & MBA

LEAD YOURSELF TO SUCCESS: YOUR GUIDE TO PROSPERITY

Acknowledgements

There are so many people to whom I owe the debt of gratitude for helping and supporting me throughout this journey. There are too many to mention by name, but you know who are. But I have one special person I want to mention by name: Mariette Francois. Mrs. Francois passed away a few years ago, but her acts of kindness and encouragement toward me while I was in Belle Glade as a farmworker and learning English shall remain with me. I wish she could read this book. She would be very proud.

And, of course, Ann McIndoo, my Author's Coach, who got this book out of my head and into my hands.

Table of Contents

Preface

In the village where I was born and grew up, education was a luxury, not a necessity. Many parents didn't understand the importance of education and didn't send their children to school. Even the Haitian government didn't understand the need to provide a system of education in order for its citizens to thrive, so there was no school in the entire village. The closest school for children to learn to read and write was approximately six miles away. Children had to walk a round trip of about twelve miles a day on rocky, dusty, muddy roads, and risked their lives to cross a lake of deep water to attend the school.

When I was about seven years old, I would walk to the rice fields with my father. On the way, we would often meet children walking to school. On our way back from the field, we would meet them coming back from school. As I continued to see them every day, I developed a deep desire to attend school like them. I kept dreaming about learning how to write my name and even the names of some of my relatives.

I remember there was a doctor who used to travel from a distance to our village to provide medical care. He carried a brief case with some medications to sell to his patients after his brief consultation and examination. In his brief case he also carried a medical book. I didn't know what kind of book it was back then. I would watch him open the book after a patient described his or her symptoms. My guess was, he was trying to determine what kind of medication to give that patient based on the symptoms described. I recall developing a strong curiosity to understand what was on the pages of that book. Even though I couldn't read, I would try to stand behind the doctor so I could glance over his shoulder at his book, trying desperately to read the written words in it. The grownups would reprimand me for trying to do that. They thought I was being rude, but they didn't know what was inside of me: the desire to learn.

A couple of older boys who lived near my house were already going to school. Whenever I got the chance, I was fascinated to listen to them, reading their books and studying their lessons. It was the coolest thing to me, and I wanted to do the same so badly.

As much as I wanted to go school, I wasn't able to communicate that desire to my father. Growing up, I didn't have a relationship with my father in which I could freely express myself. I could only speak when spoken to. As a kid, that was one of the most frustrating things to me, but I continued dreaming and nurturing my desire. Until one day, I overheard my father talking with his friend and I heard my father make a statement that surprised me. He actually said he would send me to school that year!

I thought, how could he know my desire? I had never communicated it to him. Maybe he had observed the way I looked at the other kids going to school as we were going to the fields and read my facial expression? I didn't know, but I was so happy to hear him make that statement, I didn't feel hungry all day! All I could think was, what a day that would be, when I finally attended school. My father took a bold action when he decided to send me to school. Most of his friends and other farmers didn't send their kids to school. They thought it was more productive to have their children working in the farms with them. I am very glad and grateful for that bold action he took.

I had overheard my father's statement sometime in April or May. School was already in session until June and would not re-open until September. That meant I would have to wait for five to six months for my dream to come true.

My Fight for that Early Education

My first day in school, I remember having mixed feelings. I felt happy to be in school, but on the other hand, I felt very intimidated to be among fifty other kids for the first time in my life. The teacher was also intimidating, a giant woman sitting on her wooden chair, with a whip within reach on her desk.

There wasn't a process in place to determine whether or not I could read. I was simply placed in a class with other kids close to my age. The classroom was poorly equipped with limited supplies. There was a blackboard with a few pieces of chalk. The teacher was working from a basic book to teach the students how to read. Not all of the students, including myself, had a book. She used the one on her desk to have the kids recite their lessons. Not all the kids could read at the same level and some of them were far behind the rest of the class. You could appreciate why: they didn't even have books to practice with! The teacher's educational process was mediocre at best. She would call the kids, row by row, to recite their lessons. A kid who couldn't recite his lesson, or one who tested her patience in any way, would get a whipping accompanied by verbal abuse.

Some kids knew their lessons, but they couldn't recite them because of fear of getting whipped—especially when a kid had already tested her patience and she was already upset. One day, I observed a scene I shall never forget. That scene caused me to question whether I wanted to be in school at all. While the kids were in line to recite their lessons, the kid whose turn was next urinated on himself while the teacher was whipping the kid in front of him.

That teacher usually started that process of recitation sometime in the afternoon, but she could never quite finish before the bell rang. The next day, she would pick up where she left off. Some kids would try to act smart and try to switch seats to avoid getting called on, but if they got caught, she would whip them even more severely. I spent a few weeks in that class without having any idea of what I was doing, until they finally switched me to a beginner class. There I was, probably the oldest, but I could start learning my ABCs without getting whippings by that angry teacher.

While trying to get my education, I still had the responsibility to help on the farm. I had to wake up as early as 5:00 in the morning to tend to my father's goats and cows before running to school. I left school around 3:30 in the afternoon and got to the farm around 5:00 to tend to the goats and cows again. By the time I got home to settle down, it was already dark. Given the fact that I had been up since 5:00 am, I was already tired by then. Then I would face the issue of lack of food and proper nutrition.

Although there was enough rice, vegetables, meat and fish to eat, my mother seldom ever took time to prepare meals. That wasn't her priority. I would leave home for school without eating and spend the entire day without food. Trying to learn on an empty stomach is one of the most difficult things there is for a child. It was extremely hard for me to focus. What made it worse was that I had no hope of finding food at home when I got there in the evening. I could eat my fill only during weekends or when I was not in school. During these times I would be at the farm.

It was easier to feed myself there because I had learned to cook my own food. During school hours, I was very grateful for the merchants who would come around the school during lunch time to sell peanut butter sandwiches and sugar cane. I recall one lady in particular who was selling peanut butter sandwiches. She would sell to me on credit when I didn't have the money, and I would try to pay her the next day. I was very blessed to have a kind godfather who sometimes gave me a few coins in the morning as I met him on my way to school.

Because of the long walking distance to the school and farm chores to do, time to study was very limited. I would try to study during the weekends while I was at the farm, and under a small gasoline lamp at night, but I couldn't do much studying. My eyes got tired very quickly because of the smoke from the burning gasoline.

My father made the necessary arrangements for me to attend school, but it was totally up to me to go. If I decided not to go to school for a day or week, it would not be a problem. He would not prevent me from going, but he wouldn't force me to go either. In fact, there was plenty of work for me to do at the farm. My mother, on the other hand, had other plans for me. She wanted me to carry her merchandise to the market place instead of attending school. As a result, we didn't get along at all. That was probably why she didn't care about feeding me. Learning to read and write was what I desired above anything else. I would get very rebellious when any conflict with that desire was presented to me.

As hard as it was to learn, my spirit was willing to fight and pay the price. I didn't even understand the real importance of school at that time. How could I? I was only a kid. All I remembered was my burning desire to be more than just a farm boy planting rice, chasing goats and cows. There is nothing wrong about growing rice and raising cows, except that wasn't what I wanted to do.

I believe that we are all born with that spirit of wanting to be and do more. We are born with the ability to dream. In my case, the dream was to be more than a farm boy. My dream was to learn to read and write, and believe me, that was a significant dream. Without that dream realized, you would not be reading the book you have in your hands. Many of the men in the village where I was born and raised never had the privilege to learn to read and write, even their own names. In the culture around me, I was swimming upstream.

If all of us are born with the ability to dream, and if we had many dreams when we were kids, why have only a small percentage of us achieved those dreams? *Because as we grow older, we become conditioned by society to go in the opposite direction.* For example, if I allowed my mother to pull me in the direction she wanted me to go, I would never be the person I am today. Society leads us to believe that our dreams are too big for us and that we don't have the resources to achieve such big dreams; that our educational background is not sufficient for us to do this or that.

And the resistance, the struggles, and life difficulties kill our dreams.

The truth is: you can achieve any dream as long as you are willing and able to pay the price for what you want.

Yes, I am telling you the price to achieve your dream can be very expensive and even sacrificial, but the rewards are great. I am speaking from experience. The choice I made to follow my dream of learning to read and write became the foundation of my success in life. In this book, I will show you the path I followed to create the life that I was meant to live. If you make the decision to act on the ideas you discover in this book, you will see the possibility of creating your own path to a better life.

CHAPTER ONE

Principle #1: Make Yourself Valuable

"If you want to be successful,
become a valuable person."
– Pierre St Jean

"Stop! Stop the machine!" Yelled the field crew leader, "we are leaving too many ears of corn behind! Ladies! You are not packing the corns correctly! You are not putting the required number of corns in the boxes!" The machine stopped and all was quiet. My follow Haitians looked around confused because they had no idea what the crew leader was yelling about and why the machine had stopped. They didn't understand what was going on.

Even the man who was the field walker and was supposed to translate was confused; he also didn't completely understand what the crew leader had just said and why the machine stopped. Suddenly, without any hesitation, I spoke and translated what the crew leader had said from English to Creole. The workers acknowledged with a nod of understanding and the crew leader breathed a big sigh of relief.

At last, one of us understood him. That was my second season in the cornfield, and it was my goal to teach myself to speak English. I was not quite there yet, but I was definitely making progress. My ability to speak and understand was good enough to translate. With my heavy Creole accent, I continued to translate the communications from English to Creole and Creole to English between the crew leader and my fellow Haitians during the remaining hours for that day.

At the end of that day, the members of the crew got paid forty-five dollars each, but I received sixty-five dollars. That was forty-four percent more than the other members received. Not only that, I was appointed the official language facilitator for the crew and the field walker. Essentially, my job at that point was to continue to translate the communication and walk behind the crew members to make sure that they wouldn't leave any corn behind. As a result of that promotion, *I earned more money and worked less.*

The process of harvesting sweet corn involved a crew of about twenty workers, stripping the corn off the stalks and throwing them onto a moving belt where another twenty workers standing on a mule train packed the freshly picked ears of corn into boxes. A crew leader communicated with the farmer and I communicated with the crew.

Many of the immigrant workers who pulled the ears of corn from the stalks, and the other workers who packed the corn in boxes, were Haitians who did not speak or understand English. The crew leader, who didn't speak Creole, had great difficulty communicating with the workers and that barrier of communication was causing confusion and chaos in the process.

Every ten to fifteen minutes, the mule train had to stop. As a result, we were not pulling and packing as much corn as we should, and our crew was making less than average money compared to what the other crews were making. My ability to speak and understand sufficient English at that point allowed me to solve that serious communication problem.

From the day I solved the communication problem until the end of the season, I didn't have to wake up early and walk to the loading ramp every morning to catch the bus to the farms. The crew leader drove his pick-up truck to the camp where I slept to pick me up. I became a very valuable member of the crew. The entire crew needed me because of the value I added to the process.

In your Creator's eyes, you are very valuable. There is no other life more valuable than yours. All of us, as human beings, have the same intrinsic value before the Creator. As far as He (your Creator) is concerned, your value does not increase or decrease based on the marketplace; however, society judges and compensates you according to the value you bring to the marketplace, the quality of product or service you create, and how much value you add to society and other people around you.

Thus, based on the societal standard, your value can be increased or decreased depending on the superiority of your product or service. In that respect, the degree of your financial success is dependent on how valuable you are as an individual. You can think or say whatever you want, or blame anyone or anything you want, but you are not going to achieve any level of success until you can develop yourself to be a valuable member of society. The society does not respect nor pay attention to you if you don't bring any value to the table. It always rewards the winners not the losers. Watch any game or competition to remind you of this simple fact: the trophy always goes to the winner.

Develop a Greater Version of Yourself; One of The Principles that will Revolutionize Your Financial Success

The way you become more valuable is by developing a greater version of yourself. We are the only creatures, that I know of, who are created with the capability to alter and improve their environment. We are capable of developing a greater version of ourselves and improve the condition of our lives. We learn how to build shelter to keep us warm and safe; we learn how to build fire; we have invented electricity, computers, and smart phones; we dominate the marine and the air space. I don't think we have any limit. Only God Almighty can stop you.

We may *choose* not to develop a greater vision of ourselves to earn more than the minimum wage in the marketplace, but all of us have the potential to do more, be more, and certainly to earn more income.

At one point in my life, I truly felt I was condemned to a life of poverty. I was wondering, *would I ever be more than a farmworker? Is there any possibility of moving upward, economically?* But everything changed when I decided to honor my desire to teach myself to speak and read English and develop a greater version of myself.

Listen to Your Discontent

It is normal that when we feel physical pain to pay attention because our body is trying to tell us that something may be wrong. For some people, they will automatically seek pain relief or consult a doctor because, not only do we not like to be in pain, if we don't take the necessary steps to correct whatever is causing the pain, it can lead to a more serious problem.

Similarly, sometimes we feel something is wrong with our lives. We can feel discontent, we feel unhappy, and unsatisfied with life. There can be many reasons for experiencing the feeling of unhappiness and discontent, but if your feelings have more to do with the dissatisfaction with the status quo of your life, it is a good indication that you deserve something better and you are designed for something greater. Some people resent or try to avoid their feelings of discontent. It is wrong. You should, instead, welcome it and deal with it.

Your discontent can be a good indicator that the Creator is trying to communicate to you that you are more than you think you are, and that there is a greater version of yourself waiting to be developed. I believe that your darkest moment can be the most profound moment in your life because it may be the moment that God shows up to show you the way. In fact, many people don't feel the need to take the steps to change their lives until facing the most painful moment in their lives.

Let me Tell You about the Painful Moment that Transformed My Life

On a hot, June afternoon, I was in the middle of a cornfield with twenty other crewmembers in Georgia, harvesting sweet corn. It felt like the temperature could easily have been one hundred degrees.

The sweltering heat was coming from the hot sun above as well as the soil itself that was baking in the sun. We were walking behind a mule train with a running engine as we tossed the harvested corn onto a moving belt. Women were packing it into boxes (a mule train is a large engineered machine used to harvest sweet corn). The heat coming from the engine's exhaust made conditions even worse.

Any of us could have suffered from heat stroke if the crew leader didn't stop the mule train occasionally so people could drink water and run under the trees for shade. I personally knew a fellow immigrant farm worker who became paralyzed due to heat stroke while harvesting sweet corn under these conditions.

That day, I developed an allergic reaction to the pesticides sprayed in the cornfield, which caused a bad rash on my arms and neck. My rash lasted for a couple of days and it was getting worse. I couldn't be treated as I had no access to healthcare. However, one of the ladies among the crew told me to apply baby powder on the rash. Although I applied the powder, I still spent the night scratching. I stayed home for a day, but the rash didn't dry out completely and back to work with the rash and the hot sun.

During that night of scratching, although the room was very quiet, I could not sleep. Everyone else was asleep which made it the perfect time to think and reflect about the fact that I didn't like the condition of my life. I was a poor and uneducated immigrant farm worker.

I looked at the lives of my fellow immigrants who had been doing similar work for five to six years before I joined them. Not only had their energy been depleted, but they were living below the poverty level. They couldn't afford to live in a decent neighborhood where their children could attend good schools. They didn't earn enough to save for medical emergencies or any disaster.

If there was a poor farming season because of bad weather conditions, or anything to cause the loss of crops, immigrant farm workers would endure intense financial hardship because they didn't have any money saved to survive a season without work. In case of catastrophe, they were totally and completely dependent on the government and society.

They were working without any retirement plan. Once their energy was fully used up and they were of no use to the farmers, the system would spit them out without any life support. They were among the poorest, and on the bottom of the social economic level. I realized that I was rehearsing for the same life. In just a few years, my life would be exactly as theirs.

I continued with the same line of thought knowing that if I continued as an immigrant farm worker, I would be condemning myself to a life of poverty, but it wasn't yet clear to me that I had any real alternative. It was a moment of dark despair for me. Around two in the morning, I started feeling dizzy and my head was getting heavy. I was about to fall asleep when I felt a small, gentle voice whisper to my soul, *"You were born to live a better life and to make great contributions to society"*.

I was still unsure how that would ever be possible given my circumstances. There I was, just a farm worker, an undocumented immigrant, little education, no employable skills, and didn't even speak English. Logically, the idea that I was destined to make a great contribution in society didn't make any sense. I heard and believed that promise because I trusted the voice that spoke to me.

Then, I felt maybe it was possible to create a better life, and I felt a great desire to learn English and maybe I could learn a trade and technical skill to qualify me for another line of work for a better wage. *Wow! What a revelation!* Just a moment ago I was feeling sorry for myself, and now I am experiencing a completely new feeling of hope. That great desire led me on the search. What I discovered was that to learn a trade for that better job, I needed a high school diploma or its equivalent. I honored my desire and taught myself English, and that was the beginning of the process of developing a greater version of myself and that revolutionized my financial success. At any given moment in life, we have all experienced the feeling of a great desire that, maybe, we can have more than what we have, be more than what we are, or do more than what we are doing. Is there any great desire burning in your mind, in your heart, to do something great? Have you been ignoring that desire? When you experience that great desire, you have to honor it and feed it until you fulfill your destiny.

It was twenty years later when I stood in courtrooms defending homeowners against the lenders trying to throw them out of their houses, that I understood what that voice told me when He said I was born to make a great contribution. Prior to that night, I didn't see any possibility to learn English while I was in the farm labor camp because there was no school or facility available. I thought I wouldn't learn English until I left the fields in Belle Glade to another city that had better opportunities for immigrants.

The danger to this thought was that I might never leave Belle Glade like many of my fellow immigrant farm workers who got trapped and never left. But I left the corn season with a strong determination to find a way to learn English, and the only possibility was to teach myself.

Applying that effort to learn English would later qualify me for the promotion as a field walker, language facilitator, and the possibility to study and pass the GED test to attend college, and eventually became a practicing attorney. You can read the full story in my book, *From an Immigrant Farm Worker to a Lawyer*.

Your Creator Sees and Hears You Whoever You Are

The most important secret to learn is that your creator sees and hears your cry whoever you are, whether an immigrant farmworker, or in any other unfulfilling, low-wage job you may currently be stuck in.

God is still in the business of speaking to his children. He may be trying to whisper to your heart right now and communicate to you the need to develop a greater version of yourself and to become more valuable.

Working Hard is Not Enough

Financial success is not just working hard. There are many hardworking people who are poor. Working hard is a necessary factor to achieve financial success, but it is not enough. To earn more money in the marketplace, you need to develop yourself personally and learn the necessary skills to create more value.

I couldn't have earned more money by performing the same task as the other twenty workers because we all got paid equally based on the number of boxes of corn that had been pulled and packed for that day. Even if we got paid based on individual performance, it was certain some of the other workers would outperform me based on their physical strength and energy. *The only way I could earn more money was by performing a more valuable and superior task.*

Either, you are an employee or you are your own boss. To earn more, you have to add more value to the process. You cannot just ask for more. You have to prove that you are worth more. Becoming more requires that you work on yourself and get ready for the opportunity to get ahead. Working on yourself to become more is a challenge, and it requires sacrifices, but the result pays a big dividend. To be successful in life is a personal choice. It requires individual determination and hard work. No one is going to do it for you. It is your responsibility to do everything in your power to make yourself valuable to become important enough.

Solving a Problem = Increases Your Earning Power

The road to financial success requires the capacity to earn more money based on the ability to solve certain problems.

You can increase your earning power by acquiring better skills and superior knowledge to perform superior tasks that will result in better performance and more production. Anyone can earn more and have more if they take the time to develop their talents and skills to do more and be better, but it is all starts with working on yourself.

When we face the challenges and take time to develop ourselves, we acquire the skill and ability to solve problems in the marketplace and that is how we increase our earning power. *When I stumbled on this key to financial success as a result of my experience in the cornfield as a farm worker, I sensed that my life would never be the same because I suspected that I had discovered one of the combination codes of financial success.*

As a result, I never stop learning and improving myself, and as I continued to learn, I confirmed my suspicion that the way people got rich is by solving problems. Problems are everywhere; there are legal problems, housing problems, business problems, financial problems, relationship problems and many more. Anyone who can develop the skill to solve any of these problems can become a valuable person and get very wealthy in the process.

You should not worry about your national origin, your skin color, or the language you speak. Instead, you should concentrate on learning which one of the societal problems you can solve. Once you learn how to solve a specific problem, people will look for you, and society will recognize and pay attention to you.

Develop the skills or knowledge that, when people have a problem in that particular area, you are the first person they think of. If you are in a certain profession, master that profession. The better you can perform, the more valuable you are. It does not matter in what profession you are, people in the top twenty percent of your field will earn more than the eighty percent in the bottom. To become more valuable, your goal is to be in the top twenty percent in your field. It may take you years to get there, but as long as you are committed to self-improvement, you will eventually get there. If you are in a profession you do not like, it is important that you find the profession you like, and commit to be in the top twenty percent. This will make an incredible difference to you in your future.

There are many known examples of people who became rich by creating valuable products and services to the society. For instance, in the late 1800s, there was Andrew Carnegie. He revolutionized the American transportation system by the expansion of the railroads.

We also had Henry Ford, who made it possible for common individuals to own private transportation. A more recent example is the expansion of technology. All the architects of these expansions added great value to society, and they got rich in the process.

I am sure that you are already achieved some level of success – everyone does. But what you should be thinking now is how to achieve more. The process is easier than you think. Just think in terms of what skill or specialized knowledge you can develop to make you more valuable. In fact, try to develop the special skill to solve a big problem, or a problem in which a solution is very rare. Society won't stop chasing you to make you famous and rich.

Self-Discovery

"Know thyself," said the Greek Philosopher, Socrates. The best way to know yourself is through a self-discovery process. What are some unique personalities or qualities that you possess? And how do you apply these personalities or qualities to support and inspire other people around you? What activity inspires you to be so fully engaged that you don't even realize the passing of time?

What do you love to do that you would do anyway, even if you don't get paid to do it? Everyone is born with an innate talent. Some people have more than one, but everyone has at least one. Once you find your innate talent and develop it to do what you do better than anyone else, you should achieve the level of success you want; you can never truly be successful outside of your natural talent. You may earn a living, but not be truly satisfied and successful.

"Everybody is a genius, but if you judge a fish by its ability to climb a tree, the fish will live its whole life believing that it is stupid."
– Albert Einstein

Discover and Unlock Your Natural Talent

Not everyone knows who they really are and what natural talents they were born with. Life would be much easier for them if they really knew. Knowing yourself is important. People are spending time and energy on jobs and professions that are not in line with their calling. That causes a lot of frustration and unhappiness.

The best prescription for failure is trying to be someone you are not. You can never be a person that you were not created to be. You cannot be authentic by pretending. You have to be natural. The difficulty that some people have is that they never stop to reflect on who they really are. As a result, they are going through life not truly living the life they are meant to live.

They are working hard and keep failing because they are working against their natural potential. If only they had the courage to question themselves, life would be much easier on them. Whatever you are doing, to be great at it, it has to come from within.

They say all great things begin from the inside. The secret to getting rich is to develop what you are wired to do. You cannot be successful if you are not good at what you do, and you cannot be your best at what you do if it is not what you are wired to do. How can they be good at what they do if what they are doing is not in line with their innate potential?

Your Creator gives you your talent to make contributions to other people's lives, but your talent is also your means of success. You don't have to be gifted in sport or music to use your talent to create wealth. If you are gifted as a mechanic or carpenter, there is no reason for you not to develop your talent to be rich.

Your pathway from poverty to prosperity is to unlock and develop your natural talent. If you don't have the capacity to earn money, you are a poor person, and you shouldn't complain about it because the power to change that is in your hands. This is why it is so critical to discover who you are and what you are wired to do in life.

The road to financial success is not paved just for a few and the fortunate. The secret is to find what you are wired to do, to do it in a way that adds value to other people, and to get rich doing it. Your natural talent is the source of your wealth. You were born with it and it has the potential to make you rich.

The problem is that some people have neglected to develop their natural talents, but they are trying to develop the talents they wish they had. Many people are applying their natural talents, adding value to the society, and getting rich every day. Everyone on this planet has at least one natural talent.

In fact, many people who are poor are sitting on millions of dollars of talent or ideas. They may start a career or work a job just to pay the bills, but it never occurs to them to search and discover their natural talent and develop it. I suspect that one of the possible reasons is that they have never been taught or encouraged to make that discovery.

If you really want to become wealthy, the first place to start is discovering and unlocking your natural talent. You should spend time to discover your natural talent at the earliest possible time to avoid wasting time and resources in a career that will never make you wealthy.

Each one of us on this planet is fully equipped with a specific talent to make some specific contributions to society and become rich in the process. If you don't believe me, look around, wherever you are. Everything you see, touch, and use right now, has been created by someone just like you who has discovered and unlocked his or her natural talents.

Develop Your Skill

A talent is something you are born with, but a skill is something you develop. In fact, you have to develop your talent into skill. If you have an undeveloped talent, it doesn't do you any good. You need to commit to developing it. You should be prepared to make any sacrifice to be good and excel at what you do, and to be the best at it. *The way that you are going to earn the highest possible income is being the best at what you do.* You don't even need to worry about competition if you are the best at what you do.

Getting Rich is Not Impossible, But There is a Price to Pay

You pay the price either way. You can pay the price to be rich or pay to be poor. The only difference is that the price to be poor is way more expensive. If you want to be rich, you have to pay the price in advance to be trained and develop your talent to be more valuable. If you don't pay the price to be rich, you will pay the price to be poor for the rest of your life. Even if an immigrant comes to the United States with no English speaking ability, no job skills, and with less than a high school education, if they commit to mastering the English language, earn a high school equivalent education, continue their education and develop their talents and skills, they can now can enjoy a higher standard of living. This is a right they earned through sacrifice and delayed gratification.

Value to Yourself = Value to the Society

You add value to the society when you invent a good product or perform a valuable service. For example, by facilitating the communication among the crew leader and my fellow immigrant farm workers, the crew performed better, more efficiently, and harvested more corn. The crewmembers earned more money as a result and the farmers increased their profit margin because of an efficient process.

When Steve Jobs introduced the iPhone in the marketplace, internet became available everywhere. That brought communications and commerce to a higher level. A few years ago, I was in the remote location in Haiti where I was born and raised. One of my nephews pulled out his smart phone and called his father who was in the United States.

When I was my nephew's age growing up in that remote location, access to this kind of communication was not even imaginable. My nephew can also download apps via his smart phone to learn English or any other language he wishes to learn. He can also improve his skills in math, reading, and science. He can buy and resell any product he wants to make money. Others will still come and improve on what Steve Jobs did, but his name will always be mentioned in the history books.

Invest in Yourself

Developing a greater version of yourself requires that you continue to invest in yourself. Self-improvement is one of the most important investments you can make. You should never satisfy or become complacent at your current level. You have to make a decision to develop your best self.

Life is like a race, and you are in it automatically. In the race, there are winners and losers. You don't have to be one of the losers, but if you stop improving yourself, you are lagging behind, and running the risk of losing the race. Are you running to win?

Make a Commitment to Expand Your Mind

Some people are very committed to physical development, building strength and muscles. It is very important to be physically healthy. Our health should be one aspect of living a balanced life, but some people neglect the other aspect of personal development: their mind. Look, you have to make it a practice to read one or two books per month in the area of your field to expand your mind.

Now it is easier to read than ever. There are all kinds electronic devices available to listen to books while driving, cooking, exercising, and while doing almost anything. There is zero excuse! In addition, you can register and attend classes, seminars and workshops being offered.

Self-improvement and continuing education is a life-long commitment. Even if you are in your profession for twenty to thirty years, you still can learn from speakers, teachers and mentors. In fact, listening to other speakers is one of the best ways to learn to build and expand on your own ideas.

Demand More of Yourself

If you honestly want to develop a greater version of yourself, you need to demand more of yourself. People don't just become successful. There is a price to pay to become a person of value. You have to develop different habits and do something different than your average friends.

> *"For things to change, YOU have to change.*
> *For things to get better, YOU have to get better.*
> *For things to improve, YOU have to improve.*
> *When YOU grow,*
> *EVERYTHING in your life grows with you."*
> *– Jim Rohn*

You may have to watch less television, and sometimes even get less sleep. You have to raise the bar and set a higher standard for yourself. The difference between the successful and unsuccessful people is that the successful people will do whatever is morally and legally possible to get what they want, but the unsuccessful people will do only what is convenience and easy.

Develop the Audacity of a Greater Expectation

For people who were born and raised in the environment with limited access to education and other resources, it may be hard for them to expect much from life because they may have already developed a limited mindset. Their environment and conditions may already place them in boxes of limitation. For example, you may grow in an environment with no encouragement to fulfill your destiny. In fact, not much was expected of you. It is easy for you to accept to remain in that box of limited expectation that you have been placed in. To get out of that box, you need to make a conscious effort to develop an audacity to expect more from life. In life, you don't always get what you want or deserve. *You get what you expect, ask, and negotiate for.*

Jesus said, "Let it be done to you according to your faith," (Matthew 9:29). Here, in this verse, faith can be translated as an expectation. In fact, according to Hebrews 11, faith is a firm expectation of what you want. Some people remain in certain financial conditions because they have accepted it.

They never expected their conditions to change; however, they can change their conditions by changing their expectations. Because of the pre-conditioning mindset, we have developed habits of low expectations. According to the law of expectations, whatever you expect becomes your reality.

If you don't expect to accomplish big things, you won't, but if you can develop the audacity to expect to be great, you will be. For example, if you desire to earn a certain yearly amount of money so you can access good healthcare for your family, good education for your children, and have enough financial resources available for when you can no longer work, you can set the expectation to achieve these goals by doing the things that requires to earn that certain amount of income.

One way to accomplish this is to develop your talents and abilities to the highest level to bring a product or service to the marketplace that will earn the highest income. You can activate your faith and send a direct message to your subconscious that you mean business. Eventually, that expectation to earn sufficient income to live the life you want will become your reality. Take the steps or actions that will lead you to success. You can talk about success all you want, but you don't meet with success until you take the necessary steps or actions.

Success or failure is nothing but self-fulling prophecy. People who expect to succeed, will. People who don't develop that positive and optimistic attitude of expectation of success, they tend to fail. You create that audacity of expectation by the way you think life should be for you and the way you think you deserve to live.

If you don't have the training or education you need to succeed, you go get it, succeed you must. You should never settle for less than you deserve. You may not succeed the first or the second time, or even after many attempts, but if you expect to succeed, you don't quit.

> *"Our greatest weakness lies in giving up.*
> *The most certain way to succeed is always to*
> *try just one more time."*
> *– Thomas Edison*

Self-Confidence

Successful people have high self-confidence. You were born with full self-confidence to conquer the world, but you lost your self-confidence as a result of negative conditioning by your environment. You can take back your self-confidence by reprograming yourself. Your subconscious mind has been programmed to give you certain results. To get a different result, you need to re-program your subconscious mind.

To explain the reprogramming process, let's use the computer analogy. A computer is programed to work perfectly and does so until it is infected by a virus. No matter how powerful and fast a computer is, once the virus takes over, you cannot make it do anything. A computer technician needs to remove the virus, clean the system, and reprogram it.

The same process of reprogramming your subconscious mind is necessary to achieve the result you want. Low self-confidence is one of the worst viruses any mind can get infected with, and our environment is working overtime to infect our minds with this type of virus.

"Many people have failed to achieve anything significant in their lives, not because of a lack of desire to be successful, but because they failed to develop a sufficient amount of self-confidence to go after what they want," (Pierre St Jean, *From Immigrant Farm Worker to Lawyer*, 2018).

How well we do in life is very dependent on our self-confidence. If our confidence is low, we will not set and achieve any goal. We may not even try. Once you believe that you cannot achieve a goal, there is a good chance that you won't. Henry Ford famously said, *"Whether you think you can or whether you think you can't, you are right."* But whatever goal or desire your Creator places in your heart, it is achievable. You just need to develop enough self-confidence to go after it.

One of our most famous American inventors, Thomas Edison, had very high self-confidence. Regardless of how many times he failed, because of his strong confidence in his ability to try, try, and try again as many times as it took, he succeeded in the end. People with high selves-confidence never quit because of failures, instead, they used their failures as learning tools to do better the next time.

If you have a hundred percent assurance that you will find gold at a specific location, how much digging would you do before you quit? Of course, the best answer is you will never quit because you have a hundred percent assurance that the gold is there. Similarly, you cannot fail if your self-confidence is at a hundred percent. You will try as many times as it takes. The point is, when your self-confidence is high, you have the courage to overcome obstacles in order to move forward.

Face Your Fears

Fear is a strong factor that affects self-confidence. We all have many fears: We are afraid of criticism. We fear that we are not good enough. We fear that we can't do certain things. We fear that we don't have the money or the resources to do what we would want to do. We are afraid that we may fail if we try.

For me, my fear was that my education level was too low to be more than a farm worker, and my English could never be good enough to earn a GED or diploma. Prior and during my law school journey, my fear was that I was not law school material and I could never succeed in law school. Looking at my background, you could probably draw the same conclusion that I didn't stand a chance of being a lawyer.

My fear was an inferiority complex because I was being programed to think I was inferior. Fear is nothing but a mental feeling. If you face it, you will overcome it because you are stronger than it.

Because of fear, some people don't make decisions looking at what's possible. Instead, they make decisions based on their current conditions. Their line of thinking is they could do something *if* their conditions were different. As a result, they never accomplish what they love or become successful.

You will rarely have the perfect conditions to start anything. Your thought process should be: "I love to do _____, what are the possibilities available to me right now? For example, when I had the desire to learn English, if I had waited until there was an available school, I probably would never have learned to speak English.

Many of my fellow immigrant farmworkers never learned. But by deciding to take advantage of what was available to me, such as a library, dictionaries, and some books to read, that decision transformed my life.

How Do You Build Your Self-Confidence?

The best way to start building your self-confidence is to find your purpose in life. We will talk more about your purpose later, but all I want to say for now is that, once you know why you are doing a certain thing, your self-confidence increases.

You need a true assessment of yourself. Be honest with yourself. If you need additional education or training, go get it. You gain self-confidence by harnessing your talent, acquiring knowledge and experience. Self-confidence is not pretending to know what you don't know, or "fake it until you make it" as the saying goes. It is foolish to walk in the darkness. You should, instead, have full confidence in your ability to research and learn what you don't know.

The Source of Your Self-Confidence

Some people make the mistakes of relying on their training, intelligence, as important as it is to believe in your ability to succeed (self-efficacy), but Your God should always be the source of your total expectation. Your intelligence, education, training, and experience are not enough. People who don't acknowledge their creator as their total source of dependence never finish well.

"Trust not in your own understanding; instead, trust in God with all your heart". "In whatever you do, rely on Him, and He will lead your steps," (Provers 3: 5-6).

Jeremiah 17 says we should not trust our mere flesh. Palms 62 says, "My soul waits only upon God" and "My expectation is from Him".

Poverty is a Lack of Pro-Action

According to Merriam-Wester, poverty is the state of not having a usual or socially acceptable amount of money or material possessions, but based on my experience as someone who was born and raised in a poor country, and a former immigrant farmworker here in the United States, I believe that we have two types of poverty in the world.

The first is: Absolute poverty, where people don't have enough resources for their basic needs such as: food, shelter, clothing, and basic medical care.

The other type of poverty is what we define as relative poverty. This type of poverty occurs when someone cannot afford a certain minimum of living standards. In my opinion, both types of poverty can be eradicated.

I experienced the first type of poverty, both when I was growing up in Haiti, and as an immigrant farmworker in the U.S.

Absolute poverty can be eradicated by societal intervention, but it has to be done the right way.

Relative poverty can be eradicated by taking personal responsibility where each individual takes full responsibility to earn sufficient income to enjoy the standard of living that individual wants.

A man is not necessarily poor because of his environment or disabilities. Society is full of people with extreme disabilities who are making millions of dollars. A man may be poor or rich based on his thinking. A person can bring himself out of poverty by applying the right self-empowering thought process. A person is not necessarily limited by resources or lack of opportunities, however, he or she may be limited by his or her imagination.

Some People May Be Satisfied with Temporary Assistance

There is no lack of debates on how to eradicate poverty. The United Nations debate it, United States and other countries debate it. Even the churches are debating the issue of poverty and how to eradicate it, but to successfully eradicate poverty, we need to attack the cause of it. Some people and countries may be satisfied with temporary assistance from others.

The temporary help can temporarily alleviate the pain of the people, but it does not attack the cause of the poverty. In fact, some of the so-called help may even prevent people from taking charge to develop better versions of themselves. The temporary assistance they are receiving can cause them to develop a mindset of dependency.

My idea is that any form of help should be genuinely based on a process of wealth creation, such as helping the individual to develop a specialized skill to produce value. That does not mean I am against all form of temporary assistance. In case of a natural disaster, for example, some temporary assistance may be necessary to help people to get back on their feet, but that is as far it should go. I am against of all form of perpetual assistance to anyone who is physically and mentally capable to be a producer of their own success.

CHAPTER TWO

Principle #2: A Definite Vision

"Where there is no vision, the people perish"
– (Proverbs 29:18 KJV).

Success does not happen by accident or chance. It has to be designed and made. To succeed in life, you have to be a visionary. You need a personal vision with a master plan, and your master plan needs to start with a definite and specific vision. You need clear goals, a detailed plan of action, and specific timelines to achieve each goal toward fulfilling your vision.

Define Your Vision

Your vision must be clear and definite. It cannot be vague and ambiguous. When your vision is clear and specific, you know exactly where you are going and what to do every step of the way. When defining your vision, this is where you decide what you really want. What kind of person you want to become and what value you want to bring to the society. You don't have to know all the details and how you will actually fulfill your vision. Most people cannot clearly define their vision because they are thinking based on their circumstances, not based on what their creator places in their hearts.

When I left the cornfield in Georgia, I had no idea how I was going to make the transition from an immigrant farm worker to the person I became today, but through some Divine way, which I may never understand, that vision was fulfilled. The Bible says, *"Men plan their lives, but God leads their steps."* You are capable to be and do more than you think. All you have to do is taking the first step in obedience, and your creator will lead you.

If you have a definite vision with precise and clear goals, the possibility of reaching your full potential is more certain. Vison is so critical, the only person who is a failure is a person without a vision; take someone with nothing but a vision and you have someone who can succeed.

"Where there is no vision, the people perish,"
(Proverbs 29: 18 KJV).
– King Solomon

Solomon was a very wise king. He became king when he was very young, with limited experience, and he was not sure how to carry out his kingly duties. He had to lead and administer justice over a large group of people. God appeared to him in a vision and told him, *"Ask me anything you want, and I will give it to you."*

He thought about the tremendous task of leadership before him and concluded that there was one thing he wanted: wisdom. "Now, LORD, my God, you have made your servant king in place of my father, David. But I am only a little child and do not know how to carry out my duties."

"Your servant is here among the people you have chosen, a great people, too numerous to count or number. So, give your servant a discerning heart to govern your people and to distinguish between right and wrong. For who is able to govern this great people of yours?" The Lord was pleased that Solomon had asked for this (1 Kings 3:7-10 NW).

During Solomon's reign as king, he displayed his wisdom in his ruling when he settled a dispute between two women claiming to be the mother of a child. You can read the full story in (1 Kings 3: 16-28), his ruling is one of the most critical decisions in the history of jurisprudence. The point is that Solomon's wisdom is so profound; his insight concerning life is worth following.

There is power in your personal vision

Once you discover your vision, all the forces of the universe are conspired to help you succeed. If you can dream something, you can achieve it. Create an image of the person you want to be and keep that picture in your mind until you become that person. Walk around and conduct yourself as the person you imagine to be.

Have you ever heard people say someday they will do this or that, but that someday never comes? That someday is today. If you don 't do it today, you may never do it. People shouldn't procrastinate doing what they should do to succeed in life. *"Hope deferred makes the heart sick, but desire fulfilled is a tree of life,"* (Proverbs 13:12). Procrastination is laziness, and laziness causes poverty. *"How long will you lie there, you sluggard? When will you get up from your sleep? A little sleep, a little slumber, a little folding of the hands to rest — and poverty will come on you like a thief and scarcity like an armed man," (Proverbs 6:9-11 NW).*

Here is another piece of advice from King Solomon: "*A man who is diligent in his business shall stand before kings. He shall not stand before officials of low rank,*" (Proverbs 22: 29). A diligent person is always working with a plan and implementing his plan at the right season. Are you a diligent person?

Show Me Your Vision, I Will Tell Your Future

The same way that a tree is inside of its seed, what you were created to be is already inside of you. So, if you want to know who you are, you have to look inside of you, not at your environment and circumstances. For a seed to become a tree and produces fruits, it has to be planted. Similarly, if you want to produce fruits, you need to plant your visions and ideas. As long as we continue to breathe, we will create a future anyway.

Why not creating a productive and fruitful future? A personal vision is what gives us some level of control of what that future should be. Some people are looking for prophets or fortune tellers to predict their future, but what they fail to realize is that their future is already inside of them.

You can predict your future by creating your personal vision. Show me your vision and I can tell what your future looks like. It all starts with a vision. No one can be successful without being connected to their vision. No problem was ever solved without a vision. No great invention never been completed without it. No political, social, and economic problem can be solved without a vision.

The visionaries are those who add values to the society and make our lives better. They gave us freedom from slavery, civil rights, electricity, airplanes, medicine, and technologies.

To continue in life without a vision is a great loss of precious time. Without a vision, you will continue to live a life as it is now, with nothing to show for it on your deathbed. This is why some people are regretful at the end of their lives. They never fulfilled their true purpose in life.

Most people get trapped in poverty because of lack of having a vision for their life. Vison can break all the power of limitation and it set people free. Where there is no vision, poverty and suffering are in abundance. To win in life, you must fight with a purpose. A personal vision will give you a purpose to fight.

Some people wake up every day and navigate through life without any idea of what they have to fulfill in life. Most of the struggles in life are due to misdirected life with no personal vision.

Some people are in certain jobs or profession by default, not because it is the job that is best for them. They have careers they didn't choose — the careers chose them, and they are unhappy. Worse yet, they are still poor even when working countless hours. They are not at their best because they are not working in harmony with their vision.

Make Your Vision Big Enough to Outlive You

If you want to add value and create a fulfilling legacy for society, you need to think big. Since you are creating a vision anyway, you should make that vision as big as possible. People who are afraid to think big fail to understand one thing: The mind does not care about how big or small your vision is; it will use the same level of energy to execute your vision, big or small. It is all about the level of your faith in your vision.

Offer Your Vision to God as an Offering

Your vision should be so big that you cannot fulfill it without Divine assistance. In fact, if you can fulfill your vision without the help of the Creator, it is not big enough. After creating your vision, you should offer it to God as an offering. Ask Him to use your vision to fulfill His purpose in you. I don't know your belief, but I believe in God, and I know for sure that He is very much interested in my success and yours.

How else can you explain a farm boy who didn't learn to read until he was eight years old, who came to the United States at twenty-one with an eighth-grade level of education, but taught himself English to pass the GED while working as an immigrant farm worker, became a lawyer and successful business man, except that God is on his side?

*"For I know the plans I have for you," declares the LORD, "plans to prosper you and not to harm you, plans to give you hope and a future,"
(Jeremiah 29: 11 NW).*

What is a Vision?

A vision is what you see is possible before it becomes visible. It is not what you see with your physical eyes, rather, what you can see with your mind. This is why your vision is personal, because no one else can see it until it is being manifested, physically.

Some people are not doing more because they are limited to what their physical eyes can see; they are not looking with their hearts. Instead, they are looking with their physical eyes, which can be deceiving.

Because many people are pre-programmed by fear and limiting beliefs, our natural beings do not always reflect what we really are and what we can do or become.

Write Your Vision Down

"Write the vision and make it plain,"
(Habakkuk 2:2).

Your plan should not be complicated. In fact, it has to be plain and simple to understand and follow, but it has to be in writing.

In a research study of its MBA graduates, Harvard University reported that eighty-four percent of the class did not set goals. Thirteen percent had goals, but they were not in writing, and three percent had clear, specific goals in writing with plans of actions to achieve them. The research revealed that the three percent of students with clear, specific goals and plans of action, made ten times more money as the remaining ninety-seven percent, combined.

Other Research studies show that when people write down their goals, they increase their chances of achieving them by forty-two percent. Think about something you want, you are only using the imaginative center of your brain.

> *"Think about what you want and write it down,*
> *then you are also tapping into the power of the*
> *logically-based left hemisphere of your brain.*
> *The act of writing down what you want sends*
> *a strong signal to your consciousness and every*
> *cell of your body that you mean business."*
> *– Mary Morrissey, September 13, 2016)..*

Create A Blueprint of Your Vision to Follow

- Set SMART GOALS

- Be clear on what you want

- Go after what you want with full determination: Don't be wishy washy

A vision starts with a concept in your head, then a plan to follow, with action steps to implement which lead to fulfilling your vision. There are certain decisions you have to make like:

- Determining what you want

- Be clear and specific about what you want or where you are going;

- Determine how long it will take you to get there;

- What or how much will it cost to achieve your goal or reach your destination?

- How will you know when you achieve your goal or reach your destination?

- Finally, are you willing to pay the price to achieve your goal or reach your destination?

A blueprint of your vision will force you to address the above steps. You set a measurable benchmark and time-frame and quantify the price that must be paid to achieve each step toward your vision.

Find a Coach to Help You

Personal Coaching is a relatively new concept. When the word "coach" was mentioned in the past, people usually thought about sports. It is not until the past few years that personal coaching has become popular. A personal, business or life coach can help you objectively assess your skills and talents, help you develop your abilities as well as help you create a plan of action. A coach can help you assess what you have already accomplished and what you can do better to achieve bigger and better results.

A coach can you help to see the big picture, help you clarify your goals, and build your confidence. You may be more talented than your coach, but he or she can help you to see your blind spots and help you to become a better player and achieve more. Every successful person has a good coach or mentor to help him or her to be better at what they do.

In choosing a coach, don't just hire someone you find online. The internet is flooded with people who call themselves coaches, but they never achieved any degree of success themselves. Some of them just took a class online and get a certificate and call themselves coaches.

Keep in mind that a coach has to be someone who has experience playing and has won the same game you want to win. Check out the qualifications, experiences, and credentials. In other words, before you hire someone as a coach, you want to see his or her results of playing and winning at the game. Can you imagine hiring a football or basketball coach who never played and won a game? You will never win a championship no matter how talented your players are.

It is Never Too Late

Some people may think if they didn't achieve a certain goal a few years ago, now it is too late. People with this type of negative mindset should consider the story of Harland Sanders (known to millions as Colonel Sanders). After many years of personal and business failures, he had reached the age of sixty-five years old and was living on social security income.

It was time for him to call it quits according to conventional thinking. But instead of calling it quits, the Colonel, as he became known, created his famous chicken recipe and drove from restaurant to restaurant, covering thousands of miles until finally, he found a buyer for his chicken recipe. *He never gave up.* His relentless pursuit developed into the KFC Brand, which today employs thousands of people around the world. The Colonel died a billionaire and added tremendous value to society.

According to Forbes Magazine, KFC was number eighty-eight of the world's most valuable Brands in 2019, and the KFC Brand was valued at $8.5 billion dollars. Not bad for a man who was broke at the age of sixty-five years old and collected Social Security.

Does What You Want Align to Your Purpose?

This question is important, and it requires deep reflection. It is very disappointing to work hard for something and find out that what you got is completely wrong.

Many people in life find themselves in a position or situation that they don't like. What they got is not what they really wanted, but the truth is, whatever you got is what you decided and took action on. Where and how you live, work, and play are all directly connected to decisions you have made and took action on.

Maybe you didn't know better, perhaps you decided by ignorance, but it is yours now. Some people are spending more time fixing mistakes they made in the past because of their erroneous thinking instead of spending trying to design their next five or ten years.

Before you embark on that journey to go after what you want, it is critical that you take some time to reflect on what you really want because, if what you really want will not allow you to create the best version of yourself, it may not be the right thing. It is difficult to determine your true heart's desire because your choice could be influenced by many different outside factors, such as your parents, your friends, and your environment, or you might choose that path because you thought that was your best path of survival.

Many people are convinced to attend vocational schools and colleges to make certain career choices and end up unhappy because, upon the completion of their program, they realize they have no real passion for the vocation they studied so hard for.

Even when they are working in that profession, they may look good outside, but inside, they are not truly happy.

They are there by default, but not by the choice they made themselves according to their heart's true desire. You can never be happy and truly successful pursuing goals that are not your true passion. Some people fail miserably or get mediocre results at best because they are not pursuing their true passions.

You may spend time and resources pursuing goals and desires to discover that wasn't what you really wanted in the first place. Pursuing goals which are not your true heart's desire, are not only costly, but also delay you on your journey of success. *Taking time to think about and discover your true heart's desire and passion is a smart thing to do prior to embarking on the journey of personal success.*

Discovering Your Purpose

Your purpose is why you do what you do. If you know the reason behind what it is you want, no obstacle can stand in your way, but if you don't know or have a purpose for it, it is easy to quit when things get tough. Before going after your heart's desire, you need to discover your purpose. No one is here by accident. There is a purpose for your existence and a mission to accomplish before returning to your creator. The difficulty for some people is to discover what that mission is.

The other reason that you need to know the purpose is that you don't want to start climbing a ladder and, when you get to the top, discover that your ladder is leaning against the wrong wall. According to Stephen Covey, in his book, "7 Habits of Highly Effective People", you need to *"Begin with the end in mind"*.

If the ladder is not leaning against the right wall, every step we take just gets us to the wrong place faster. It is good to work hard for what you want, but there is nothing worse than working hard for the wrong thing.

So many people get caught up in the "busy-ness of life", but their ladder is leaning against the wrong wall. So many people are unhappy and dying with regrets because they worked hard during their entire lives climbing the ladder of success, but when they got to the top, they discovered that the ladder was leaning against the wrong wall. It makes sense to determine your purpose in life while you are at the bottom of the ladder, *before* you start climbing.

Some people never know any significant success in their lives because they never took time to consider their purpose. How do you get anywhere in life without knowing where you are going? Or better yet, how do you know when you get there, if you ever get there at all? It is no surprise that people are running around in circles without making any progress in life. They don't have a real destination.

If only they took time to examine their heart and discover their purpose, they would realize then, that they are not fulfilling their true heart's desire. Discovering your purpose can make all the difference because that is what separates those who make changes in their environment and affect the lives of people around them, and those who don't.

Discovering your purpose can also affect your financial success. For some people, even though they have certain desires, their desires are very limited because their desires are not in alignment with their purposes. They don't expect much; they are satisfied with as little as they can get. They don't have the ambition to solve any big problem although they have the potential. Environment plays a big factor.

Our environment places certain limits on what and how much we can produce. As a result, even when we have the potential, our production will not exceed the limit that is being programed in our subconscious. I was always puzzled about the fact that, in an environment full of resources, an individual would not develop any desire and follow the steps to be financially prosperous. It was not until I understood that it is a matter of mindset.

A person's desire to succeed will be in exact proportion with his or her mindset regardless of how much potential and opportunity that he or she has. Some people will even blame their failure to be financially free on their religious beliefs. Once someone is already preprogramed in a certain way, it requires a total re-programing to change that person's mindset. Until then, the person will continue to perform at the same level.

We all start with a perfect blue print. What you need to do is to learn how to access that original blue print. Once you access it and start following that perfect blue print that you were created with, you will realize that it is not about what your critics say, but it is, rather, about what your creator intended for you to be and do. Therefore, no amount of fear can prevent you from getting your heart's desire.

How Do I Know If My Desire is What the Creator's Plan for Me?

This is a very important question. Many people get stuck in life because they don't know God's plan for them. Meanwhile, life is passing them by. The fact is, I would not want to desire anything that is not God's plan for me, either.

I am not a Theologian, and when comes to the study of the Bible, I am not the person you would place in the category of an expert, but here is what I know for sure: *If what you desire will add value to other people, if it will help create a positive impact in your community and cause you to develop a better version of yourself, by all means, this is the desire you should pursue because there cannot be any better desire than that.*

I Know What I Desire, But Can I Have It?

You may doubt yourself because of fear. Fear is the number one killer of dreams and desires, but let me tell you: If you have a desire, you also have the capability to have what you desire. That desire you have is an expression of what you can become. However, whether or not you become that person or fulfill your vision is up to you, but God will never ask you to become someone you are not designed to be.

I want to construct a building. An architect has to design a plan before I can start the construction. The architect makes a detailed plan from start to finish. According to that plan, the building is already completed in the mind of the architect before we can put it in its physical form.

Similarly, your Creator is the Chief Architect of your life. You are already being designed. The person you are has already been fully completed. "For I know the plans I have for you," declares the Lord, "plans to prosper you and not to harm you, plans to give you hope and a future," (Jeremiah 29:11).

Commitment

The question is not whether you can get what you want or not, it is, rather, are you committed to getting it? Having desire and a set of blueprints is not enough. You need to take action to construct the building. You have to take action to go after what you want.

For example, if your desire is to have enough money to provide for yourself, your family, and to get your share of prosperity in the world, you can have it if that desire is strong enough and you are willing to do whatever that means legally and morally, to go after what you want. Most people don't have desires. They have wishes.

There is a big difference between wishing for something and having a strong desire for something. If your desire is strong enough, all the force of the universe will work to get you what you desire. One of the questions that you have to ask yourself is what is the reason behind the desire?

People who have reasons for their desires usually hold stronger conviction. It is important to have strong conviction when you are going after your heart's desire because you will sometimes fall. When you stumble or take a fall, you must get up and start again. Once you determine your heart's desire, and you are absolutely certain that it is what you want, you have to commit to it.

If you want something but you are not willing to make a commitment to get it, you are sending a mixed message to your brain that you are not certain of what you want. As long as you are not hurting yourself or anyone else, and you are not committing any crime, nothing should be off limit to go after.

One area in which people are having problems in fulfilling their vision and getting their heart's desire is paying the price for what they want. Fulfilling your vision and getting your heart's desire requires that you give something in exchange. What are you willing to give in exchange for what you want?

Are you willing to give up a few hours of your sleep? Or maybe give up some of your leisure time in exchange to get the desire of your heart? People ask me all the time: How did you do it with an eight-grade education at twenty-two years old? You taught yourself English and passed the GED test while working as an immigrant farm worker and worked your way upward to become a lawyer and successful businessman. I have two words: *Commitment and Discipline*. Commitment must be made, and discipline must be applied.

Success in life demands a certain price, and if success is what you want, a price needs to be paid. There is no such thing as something for nothing. You cannot expect to be successful without paying a price.

Nowadays, people spend a lot of time in front of their television set and electronic devices. These hours can be utilized to go after your heart's desire and fulfilling a vision for your life. In my book, "FROM AN IMMIGRNT FARM WORKER TO A LAWYER", I talk about commitment as one of the fundamental principles that separates a successful person from a failure. Any successful person will agree with this statement: When people are not committed, they see difficulties and impossibilities, but committed people see possibilities, and look for ways to overcome obstacles and challenges.

Whether the person is an athlete, a musician, an inventor, or an entrepreneur, he or she will practice, try, and work for as long as it takes until he or she is successful. "Our greatest weakness lies in giving up."

"The most certain way to succeed is
always to try just one more time."
– Thomas A. Edison

Many people have attempted to make the necessary changes to develop the best version of themselves, but they fall back because of fear and disbelief that they don't have what it takes to succeed. An example of that is when I was teaching myself English to pass the GED exam, there was another fellow Haitian embarking on the same project, and it didn't take long before he quit because he didn't believe that he could succeed.

Your Personal Philosophy

Over the years, you form a belief system. This set of beliefs becomes your life philosophy. The kind of habits you create, good or bad, are based on your belief system and personal philosophy. Your belief system is very powerful. It is important that you have the right philosophy because your philosophy determines the direction of your life. Unless you have the right mindset, and your belief system is in alignment with your desire to succeed, you will not make any progress.

What is your personal belief about financial success? Do you believe that only a few are destined to financially succeed? Or do you believe that each one of us regardless of his or her nation of origin has a chance to achieve financial success?

For example, do you believe that you:

- Have the right to live life to the fullest – spiritually, mentally, emotionally, and physically?

- Have the right to have enough money to access the best medical care available to you and your family?

- Have the right to good and suitable housing in a safe environment for your protection and the protection of your family?

- Do you believe that your children have the right to the same good education as everyone else's children?

- That you the right to have all the money necessary, not only to meet your own needs and to live a dignified life, but also to assist those in need? These rights are fundamental. They are given to us by our creator, not by men. You have the capability to establish and hold these rights. No one can deprive you of your right of financial independence except yourself.

How Do You Become the Person You Are?

We came on this Earth with a perfect mind, like a brand new and powerful computer fully programmed to succeed in your purpose. However, within seconds of our arrival, other people started to re-program our minds with their own programs. Some of these programs are: Fear, negative criticism, inferiority complex, not good enough, not talented enough, not enough education, feeling of incompetence, low self-confidence, jealousy of other people's success, and constantly trying to get other people's approval.

If we fail to make everyone happy, we think we are failures, and the list goes on. This negative information took over our minds like a virus taking over a computer system. This information has been installed in our brains by a combination of people who have had influence over us, such as our parents, grandparents, aunts, uncles, schoolteachers, and our peers. They all place their stamps on us in one way or another, whether we realize it or not.

Realize that this bad information they have been sowing in our minds has been collected from other people. No one is original. We are all some form of other people, duplicated. Whatever information they have been installing in our system, they got from the previous generations. For some people, they were fortunate enough to have better information installed in their minds because they were born and raised in a better environment.

But for those of us who were not fortunate to have good and positive information installed in our minds, we keep producing bad and negative results, generation after generation, especially those of us who have been born and raised in poor and unstable environments.

It is even harder. This is a fact that needs to be acknowledged and dealt with in order to move forward, and there is good news: The same way that a computer technician can perform a computer system clean up and re-install a new program, you can reset your mind and re-program the exact information you want.

How Do You Reset and Reprogram Your Mind?

I can't say it any better than St. Paul: "Don't copy the behavior and customs of this world, but let God transform you into a new person by changing the way you think," (Romans 12:2).

First, you need to become an independent thinker. You don't have to accept everything everyone is trying to dump in your mind. They say that an opinion is the cheapest commodity. Everybody has one.

Second, you need to change your environment. People who are telling you that you cannot do this or that, instead of encouraging and helping you to develop a greater version of yourself, are not fit to be your friends. They are not the people to be associated with. If you are going to fulfill your vision, there are certain people you need to dissociate with and choose other friends.

"You are the average of five
people you associate with,"
— Jim Rohn.

Change Your Limiting Beliefs

As you know, we are not just physical beings. We are also spiritual, emotional, and mental beings. As a result, we have to deal with both our inner and outer part of ourselves. Whatever is being manifested in our physical world is the mirror image of our inner-selves. There is an invisible force at work, and people act and do things according to that invisible force.

The key to developing a greater version of ourselves is to, first of all, deal with what has been going on inside, such as our fear that we are not good enough to have or to do certain things. Until we deal with our limiting beliefs, there is no amount of willpower or physical effort that can help us.

It is like a computer. It is programmed to perform certain tasks to give you certain and specific results. If you don't like what is being printed out, you don't change the printer. You change the program inside the computer instead.

We are multiple times more powerful than a computer. We can perform powerful results, but we need to program ourselves correctly. People with limiting beliefs won't even try to develop that greater version of themselves because they lack the certainty that there is a greater version of themselves waiting to be developed. For those of us who were born and raised in a poor environment and we never learned and experienced what is possible, it is even more difficult to change our belief system.

As I often say, I overcame many obstacles to develop a greater version of myself, but my biggest battle was against my complex of inferiority." However, if you want to empower yourself, it is a must to take control and develop a sense of certainty that you can develop that greater version of yourself.

CHAPTER THREE

Principle #3:
Whose Responsibility Is It?

*"Each player must accept the cards that life deals
him or her. But once in hand, one must decide how
to play the cards in order to win the game."*
*– VOLTAIRE, 18th Century Historian,
Writer and Philosopher*

You know what you want, and you have a clear vision of it.
Whose responsibility is it to have what you want? Is it the
government or society's responsibility? Don't let yourself be
deluded!

*"You can only have what you want to the extent
that you are willing to accept personal
responsibility for it. You can't hire someone else to
do your push-ups for you,"*
– (Jim Rohn).

One of the most popular messages we are getting from
the media is about wealth inequality. The richest one percent own more wealth than the bottom ninety nine percent
of the population. The rich are getting richer and the poor

are getting poorer. It has been reported that more than forty million people of the U.S. population are living at or below the Federal Government Guidelines of poverty level.

According to Washington Post, Oct. 17, 2018, 3.4 billion people, almost fifty percent of the world population, cannot meet their basic needs. I don't dispute the above statistic. I think the number of people fallen to poverty not only around the world, but also in the United States, is getting out of control, but the good news is, you don't have to accept poverty as your final condition, and the wealthier do not have a monopoly on the world resources.

Being rich or being poor is a mindset issue. You can be rich, too, if you are willing to take personal responsibility for it. America is creating an average of 1,700 millionaires per day. It has been estimated that by the 2020, there will be 3.11 million new millionaires in the U.S. Never before in history that we have created more wealth in a such rapid amount of time.

According to the Global Wealth Report 2018, published by the Credit Suisse Research Institute, the Global Wealth is $317 trillion, and U.S. has $98 trillion of the Global Wealth. If you are in the United States, you are living in one of the richest countries of the world. There is no reason not to be rich, except if you don't believe you deserve to be.

It is a reality that when it comes to the world of wealth and prosperity, we don't have equal access. For whatever reasons, some have more and better access than others. We don't have equal access to commerce, books, information, and education. Even with the proliferation of the internet, the reality still remains that not all of us have been dealt the same hand of cards. Some have better hands than others.

But you must also accept it as a reality and take full responsibility to play the hand that life deals you. Some people wish that they had better hands. Forget it. It is not going to happen. Nobody is going to trade you his or her good hand of cards. What you need to do instead is learn to be a better player.

Besides, a better hand does not necessarily guarantee that you will win, and a bad hand does not necessarily mean you cannot win. Many people with good hands are losing and others with bad hands are winning. You could have been born and raised in the perfect environment, and had access to good education, but you still can fail if you failed to take charge of your life. Regardless of the hand that life deals you, *you have to learn how to play the game to win.*

You may have had a very humble beginning, but you can still win if you understand that you are 100% in charge of your success. Winning the game has very little to do with the hand of cards you hold, and it has a lot to do with how you learn to play. Statistics show that many people inherit very large sum of money, or won the lottery, but still die poor.

Regardless of the hand that life dealt you, what you need to do is train yourself to be a better player. Among many things you can do are: Create better habits of discipline, develop a success mentality instead of a victim mentality, and accept the fact that you are 100% in charge of your success.

The rich are getting richer because they learned how to play the game and are always getting better at it. If you want to get your share of the world of prosperity, you need to start learning to play the game like your financial freedom is depending on it.

If you don't learn how to play the game of success, you relinquish your power to be dominated by those who know how the game is played. No one is responsible but you if you are not getting your share of the world's prosperity.

As I mentioned before, but I mention it here again just to underscore the point that "Success is Up to You." I didn't start learning to read until I was eight years old because there was no access to education in the village where I was born. The Haitian Government didn't even know my existence because my birth certificate wasn't recorded until I was twenty years old.

At twenty-two-years old, I still had an eighth-grade level of education. I was an undocumented immigrant farm worker, didn't speak English, and working for $30 for more than eight hours a day, and slept on a cement floor in a farm labor camp at night. However, everything changed when I took 100% responsibility for my future and determined to be a better player to win the hand of cards that life dealt me.

One of my favorite books is titled, *"If It's Going to Be, It's Up to Me: The Eight Proven Principles of Possibility Thinking"*, by Dr. Robert Schuller. Dr. Schuller was a televangelist, motivational speaker, and author. By the time I read this book in 1998, I had already led myself out of the farm work and obtained a college degree, but his message of possibility thinking motivated me to continue to move forward.

During all prior due diligence to develop that greater version of myself, I was not conscious about the principles I was applying. I was just following my intuition, and Dr. Schuler reinforced the lesson that I learned during my time as an immigrant farm worker that success is possible. All it takes is:

1. Knowing what you want;

2. Determining how or where to get it, and

3. Paying the price for it.

It is that simple. The problem with some people is that either they don't know what they want, or if they know, they don't know how or where to get it, or even worse, they don't want to pay the price for what they want.

You have to realize that if it is going to be, it is up to you. Regardless of where you are in life, it is your responsibility to search and get what you need to succeed. The sooner you accept the fact that the government, society nor anyone else owes you anything, and you are now 100% in charge for your financial success, the better off you will be because your journey to success starts when you get in the driver's seat and take the wheel.

There is only one person on earth who can break that chain of poverty and set you free financially. That person is you! As important as it is to have the right person represent us in the government, you don't have to wait until the right person gets elected for you to take responsibility to break your chain of your own poverty.

Regardless who is elected in power, you should always know that you are 100% in charge of your financial future. You may have to take a road that was never been followed before. There may not be any model or pattern to follow.

You may have to shape the road yourself, but succeed you must!

You may feel like you were born on the wrong side of the world because of your disadvantaged conditions. You were not raised in the right environment, had poor education, and were at a social economic disadvantage. You feel unlucky, and you can never catch a break. It is one bad thing after another. Some of these circumstances might be a direct result of your environment.

Some people say life is not fair. I get it because I have been there myself, regardless of your past circumstances or your history, to lead yourself to success, you need to start by letting go of all the blame and the excuses because you cannot create a pathway to success while you are nourishing a victim mentality. Think about it. Holding someone else responsible for where you are not, is not bringing you closer to where you want to be.

All you are doing is admitting that you are not 100% in charge of your life, and that you need permission from some outside factor to design the life you want. You need to reset your mindset.

"Problems cannot be solved with the
same mindset that created them."
— Albert Einstein

No matter what yesterday was, today you are in charge and are responsible for tomorrow. "You have to take full responsibility for where you are now because if you don't, ten to fifteen years from now, you will be 100% at fault for your own failure." (Pierre St. Jean, *FROM AN IMMIGRANT*

FARMWORKER TO A LAWYER, How to Live the Life You Were Meant to Live (2018)).

The Story of one of my fellow Haitian Immigrants

I met one my fellow Haitian immigrants while we were working in a fast food restaurant cleaning tables and washing dishes. He was one of us Haitians who didn't have the privilege of receiving a quality education in Haiti. However, when I challenged him to attend school, or at least to start learning English and maybe try to acquire some technical skills allowing him to develop a better version of himself, he gave me all kinds of excuses why he couldn't.

During several conversations with him, he expressed that he was not satisfied with what life had offered him. He was burnt out from working two jobs and still could not make ends meet, but he was unwilling to make the self-sacrifice to develop that better version of himself that will allow him to bring greater value to the job marketplace so he could demand a greater pay. By the time I left that job at the restaurant, I lost contact with that fellow. I hope he took my advice and developed a greater version of himself.

A person who is unhappy with the hand of cards that life dealt them but unwilling to learn how to be a better player to win the game, has not yet learned one of the basic principles of success: *Taking Full Responsibility.*

That person will unlikely attain success.

So, before you start blaming anyone or any circumstance for your misfortune, take a look back to see where you failed to take personal responsibility for yourself. Is there any area in your life you can take personal responsibility to change right now? Abraham Lincoln wisely said, "You cannot escape the responsibility of tomorrow by evading it today." All of us have both the right and the obligation to improve our quality of life.

One of the big differences between the people who succeed in life and those who don't is that the people who succeed believe that they can influence their own success in life and therefore take full responsibility for their lives. They plan and set goals. They don't live their lives by chance and by default. They don't have the victim mentality. They know that there are things that happen in life they don't have complete control over, such as natural disasters or acts of terrorism, but they develop better responses to these events when they occur.

Those who believe that their successes are completely dependent on outside circumstances hold their environment 100% responsible for their failures, not taking any responsibility themselves. They fail to realize that they are 100% in charge.

Once you believe that you are in charge and you are in the driver's seat, you can override the preconditioning programing and reprogram your system to the destination you want. No matter what happened in the past, now you have the power to produce a different result, the result you want. *Some people are not aware of the power they have to change their lives. As a result, they remain in their current conditions.*

People assume they are limited by a lack of financial resources and limited education. They are not aware of their power to break their chains and release themselves. They call that "elephant thinking". When they begin to train a baby elephant, they tie a chain on its leg and tie the chain to a pole. The baby elephant would try to get away many times, but it couldn't. As it grows older, it assumes it cannot get away. Now, as a six-ton animal, he could get away with little effort, but it never tries because of its assumption that it can't.

If you are still blaming the outside factor for your condition, you admit that you are not in charge, and that is a sad situation to allow someone else or some outside factor to be in charge of your life. The fact is, if you want to pass on the blame for why you are not living the life you were meant to live, you will find many people or circumstances to hold responsible, but these people or circumstances you think are responsible for your misfortunes don't care about what you think.

If you want something in life, you get it yourself. Booker T. Washington was born a slave, and as a child, he was assigned to hard labor to help his family to survive economically. Education was not available to black people during that time, but he worked diligently to educate himself. He took full responsibility for his success. As a result, he was able to make tremendous contribution to the improvement of black lives. You can read the full story in his classic book entitled "Up From Slavery".

For some people, life has offered them an invitation to a life of failure, but they have the choice to accept or decline. After a long day of hard work, and all your energy is fully depleted, the normal thing to do is what most people would do, go home, kick your feet up and get some rest because the same routine starts over tomorrow. But not if you want to reject the invitation to live a life of poverty and get busy creating a better version of yourself. Instead, register for a class at local college, university, or online to develop a greater version of yourself, and increase your earning potential. That road requires you to commit to being 100% in charge of your life and take full responsibility for it.

Belle Glade, Florida, is where I was living during the time, I was working on the farm labor camp. The possibility for an immigrant farmworker like me to move upward economically was very close to impossible. There wasn't even a school to learn English. However, there was one possibility: I had free access to a library.

That was one of the first positive aspects of the United States of America that caught my attention right away. Even in the middle of a farm labor camp, there was an open library from 9:00am to 9:00pm where people have access to free books to read. The problem was that looking at a bunch of books I couldn't read didn't help me. I had to create a system to help me with the process of learning English and study to pass a GED test.

The easiest book I could start with was a dictionary because I could learn the spelling and meaning of the words. I would copy the words and the meanings in my notebook. I would transfer them to post cards for carrying in my pockets. Each night before I went to bed, I would try to memorize those words.

Each morning while riding the bus to the corn or the sugar cane field and on my way back, I would continue to study the words. I caught the bus around 5:00 in the morning going to the farms from the loading ramp. I got back home around 4:00 to 4:30 in the evening. Depending on the work day, sometimes 6:00 pm. I would get to the library by

7:00 pm, sometimes earlier, when I got back from the farm early.

Amazing things happen when you take charge of your life. You can produce a result that will surprise you and others. When I set the plan to teach myself English and study to pass the GED, I thought I needed four years to accomplish that objective: Two years to learn English, and an additional two years to study for the GED test. However, within two years, I was able to teach myself enough English and passed the GED examination.

Taking responsibility for your success is critical. No one who wants to achieve anything in life can bypass that step. Now, if taking responsibility is so important to achieving success, why doesn't everyone accept and apply this principle to help create a successful life? Well, one reason is that failure can be very painful.

No one wants to admit that he or she is a failure. It is in our nature to avoid shame and disappointment. If someone admits that they are 100% in charge of their success, if they fail, there is no one else to blame. However, what most people fail to realize that they failed because they failed to take personal responsibility. It can be a painful mistake to allow chance and outside factors determine the direction of your life.

How Can You Increase Your Earning Potential?

Some people come to see me for legal advice after they had been fired from their jobs. They came to see me because they think they have been discriminated against. I don't discount the fact that people are being discriminated against all the time, and their firings are not justifiable, but sometimes the employee is simply, not a good producer.

The reality is you may get laid off or fired so the company can bring someone with the same or better skill for less pay. We can debate the moral aspect of that, but that's the way things are. You have to constantly prove your value to remain competitive and always increasing your earning power in the marketplace. The company does not *have* to keep you employed if you are not adding value.

What you need to do is constantly improve your value. For example, if you are a nurse's aide, you could upgrade yourself to a nurse. If you are a paralegal, you could upgrade yourself to a legal researcher, consultant or attorney. If you are a plumber or electrician, your aspiration could be to become a general contractor.

Many of my fellow immigrant farm workers were rehearsing the similar life of poverty who could have taken steps to break the chain of poverty, but for whatever reasons, they didn't. However, there were others who took full responsibilities to develop better versions of themselves and their lives are different from those who failed to take personal responsibilities.

I told their success stories in my previous book, "From Immigrant Farm Worker to Lawyer", but I think their stories are worth repeating here. In telling their stories, I use their first name only out of respect for their privacies.

Jean's Story

Jean could not afford to pay rent for a decent apartment while he was cutting the sugar cane, so, when the opportunity presented itself, Jean took the initiative. He learned how to operate a tractor. Now, because of his higher wage as a tractor operator, he was able to buy his own house. He could live in a better community with his children. His children could attend better schools with no violence. He could save to send his children to college to have careers and be on track to design better financial lives. Buying his own home was the first step toward his financial stability. Instead of paying rent, he began building equity in his house. Also, as a tractor operator, he has a permanent job. He does not have to travel out of the Belle Glade area looking for farm work at the end of each season.

Wilson's Story

Wilson was cutting sugar cane in Belle Glade, as well. After the farmers changed the system to use machines to cut the sugar cane, Wilson moved to West Palm Beach. He got a job in a restaurant washing dishes and cleaning at night, and he went to a technical school during the day.

Wilson stuck with it, became an electrician, and started earning a living wage. Wilson moved to Orlando, and bought a house, where he lives with his wife and children. Now, link by link, both Jean and Wilson are breaking the chain of poverty to gain their financial freedom.

The following stories are about Judith and Marie. Both Judith and Marie were not farm workers, but their stories are perfect examples of those who took full responsibility to develop better versions of themselves.

Judith's Story

When I met Judith in 2002, she was working two minimum-wage jobs, one of them was at a fast food chain. Between the two jobs, her gross income was about twenty-three thousand dollars per year. The only way she could qualify to buy an 800-square-foot townhouse was with the aid of a government grant.

Judith's ambition was to become a nurse. She set her goal, successfully graduated from nursing school and got a job as a nurse. She is earning twice the amount she was earning working two jobs in fast food restaurants. Many people who are working in low-wage jobs believe they are trapped. That is not true. You can get out if you want to.

Marie's Story

Marie, a single mother, wanted to purchase her first home. She had been taking public transportation back and forth to her housekeeping job because she could not afford a car. She was also collecting food stamps because she didn't earn enough in her housekeeping job.

Her local church hosted a course teaching people how to become a nurse's assistant or a home health aide. She could not afford the cost of the training, but with the help of family members and friends, she raised the funds to attend the training.

That training qualified her to work in nursing homes as well as in private homes with senior citizens. She doubled her earning income and qualified to purchase her first home. Now, she is a homeowner and she can afford her own automobile. She no longer collects food stamps. She is a taxpayer instead. If you admit that you are 100% in charge of your success and take full responsibility to develop a better version of yourself, the possibility to break the chain of poverty is within your reach.

All the books and formulas for success that have been written have one common denominator: *Personal responsibility*. Each one of us has to take full responsibility for our success or failure in life. At what point does someone become responsible for his or her success?

Certainly, one cannot be held responsible for the color of his or her skin, his or her country national origin, and the language he or she was taught to speak as a child. What about the fact that some of us were born in an environment with limiting or no access to education, no health care system, unstable social-political and economic environment? When does one become conscious of his or her life misfortune and decide to take full responsibility for his or her personal success?

I remembered when there was a point in my life that I started to be very dissatisfied with the hand of cards that life dealt me. Something needed to be changed. But what could I change? I couldn't change the hand of cards I had. The only thing I could do was train myself to be a better player. Once I realized I had the power and the capability to achieve whatever my heart desired, I could no longer be held captive by my past circumstances.

"Once you see what you can become,
you should never settle for less"
— Pierre St Jean.

CHAPTER FOUR

Principle #4: Self-Management

The Eight Critical Steps of Self-Management

Step 1: Manage Your time

To succeed in life, you have to be a *master* of time management. You set certain goals to achieve your vision, and each one of these goals is time specific. If you don't manage your time, you run the risk of missing them. Time is one of the most significant resources given to humankind by our Creator without discrimination or partiality.

Each one of us has twenty-four hours in a day, no more, no less, and the only control we have over that time is how we spend it. God does not allow us to save time for tomorrow. It may be easier if some days we could use only twenty hours and save four hours for the next day, but it does not work that way. Sometimes we hear people say, "I saved some time," but we cannot actually save time. All we can do is spend it, and we need to spend it wisely because it is in limited supply.

The reality is, each minute you spend is a transaction in exchange for something; either to learn something new to improve your life or for entertainment. For any of these minutes you spend, you make a tradeoff, and whatever the tradeoff is, the transaction is final. If you are not satisfied with your trade, you cannot go back and ask for a refund of your time. Each minute you spend, you will never see again in this life or the rest of eternity.

A truly disciplined person manages his or her time well. It is guaranteed that there will be a fresh refill of twenty-four hours tomorrow. Some of us may not live long enough to complete our next twenty-four hours, but if you do, you have the right to do whatever you want with your time.

You can use your twenty-four hours for whatever activities you choose. People who are not happy with their current situation can improve their lives by making better use of their time instead of engaging in nonproductive activities. Since we are spending the twenty-four hours anyway, why not spend them on some activities that will add value to our lives and help us to develop a better version of ourselves, and in turn, increase our earning power in the marketplace?

Time has a way of passing by without you noticing. The only way to get the best out of time is to use it judiciously. During my days of studying English and preparing for the GED, I made it a practice to avoid certain people because my goal was to get to the library so that I could study for three hours.

When friends or peers tried to take up too much of my time, I had to politely excuse myself from them. They were very nice people who were trying to engage in conversation, but they were interfering with *my* valuable time.

The problem with time is that it can slip away. Have you ever heard someone say, "Where did the time go?" It is true that time can simply disappear when it is wasted on useless and nonproductive activities. Other people have the ability to take your time away from you. When I first started practicing law, I had some difficulty saying no to people or potential clients.

Being a new attorney at the time, I thought it was my mission to resolve every legal issue people called me about, even when they could not pay me. As a result, I got over-committed and was unable to fulfill my own agenda and purpose.

Ultimately, I realized that I had to respect my own agenda enough to say no to other people's agendas that had nothing to do with completing my own objectives. I have created a list of ten items on my agenda that I need to do each day to work toward my goal for the week or for the month. I discipline myself to do these ten items without any compromises. Since I have implemented this system, it is rare that I don't finish the ten items on my list.

If I don't finish, it is not because of involuntary distraction. It could be that I intentionally readjusted my list to give priority to something else, but I am *consistently* in complete control of my own time. This system may seem simplistic, but it is very powerful. There is no way you won't accomplish your goal if you successfully complete small objectives every day that help you work toward that goal and fulfilling your vision.

You also need to prioritize your time – you cannot do everything at once. I tried that and it didn't work. No matter how smart you are, or how diligently you work, you will *need* to establish priorities.

Too many projects at once divide your focus. A divided mind is not as powerful as an undivided, focused mind. One of the best gifts a parent can give to their child is the gift of understanding the importance of time management. Some kids never utilize their time productively, which makes it difficult for them to succeed in college and in life in general.

Step 2: Self-Discipline

Every successful person is a person of discipline. It does not matter how smart and talented you are, without discipline you cannot accomplish much. If you are a student, you need the discipline to read and study the materials to pass the course. If you are in sales, you need to discipline yourself to make the phone calls and put in the effort. You cannot fail or succeed overnight – it takes continuous bad or good habits over time. Whether you fail or succeed depends on how disciplined you have been in going after what you want.

What is discipline? Discipline is taking control and being willing to work hard to achieve your goal. Anyone who has reached a certain level of success can tell you that discipline was a key factor for attaining his or her accomplishments. If you have the dream and the desire to reach your goal, you just need to build the bridge of self-discipline to cross over to your accomplishment.

Lack of self-discipline can hold you back. Most people have failed, not because they didn't have dreams, and not because they failed to set goals; they have failed because they lack discipline. It takes discipline to accomplish your goal. Your commitment will be tested by obstacles, barriers, and even distractions. If you don't have self-discipline, you will fail.

I have heard many excuses from people as to why they haven't accomplished anything significant. They blame their failures on many other circumstances, but in reality, it is just a matter of being self-disciplined, such as sitting down for two or three hours to study or to do the work it will take to accomplish your goal.

If someone can discipline themselves, they will be amazed to see how much they can accomplish. Without discipline, a person cannot accomplish much. During my undergraduate time in college, I had a roommate for the purpose of sharing the bills, but I had to find a new place to live. He wasn't disciplined enough to turn the television off during the time I was studying or trying to rest.

He would watch movies until two in the morning. That wasn't the life I wanted to live. He was a very smart and talented guy with a lot of dreams, but it does not surprise me to see that he has not accomplished anything. He is still working for minimum wage because he lacks the discipline to fulfill any of his dreams.

I learned that if you want to be good at self-discipline, you have to practice. It is challenging to create new habits at first, but once the habit is created, you will go on autopilot. There are two basic laws that can help explain why you can be on autopilot after the habits have been created: The first is the law of aerodynamics, and the second is the law of gravity.

For example, when an airplane is trying to take off from the ground, the law of gravity is pulling down to keep the plane on the ground, but once the airplane has built enough momentum and has taken off, the law of aerodynamics takes over and keeps the airplane in the air until it reaches its destination.

Similarly, you have to fight hard to build the good habit of self-discipline, but once you build the good habit of sitting for three to four hours of studying without any distraction, it will become so easy that you will be able to spend three, four, or even five hours studying without realizing it.

If you are a student, sometimes the hardest thing to do is crack the book open and try to make sense out of what you're supposed to understand. Especially, after a full day of hard work. When I first started in real estate, I had to make cold calls to prospects in the evening because that was the time I had a greater chance of finding someone to answer the phone.

The big challenge for me was that, in the evening, my energy level was usually not at its best, and I found myself completely disengaged; I had to find a way to re-engage. My secret was, when on the day I had to make the cold calls, I took a one-hour nap prior to engaging myself.

That usually brings my energy level up. With so many marketing tools available to target prospects, I don't think sales people are still making cold calls. But whatever you do, you may always find yourself disengaged. What you need to do is to find a way to re-engage.

The second thing to do is make a conscious decision to eliminate all distractions around you. During my first year in law school, I completely deleted television from my life.

I spent months without touching my cell phone. I did the same thing when I was preparing for the bar exam. I created and lived in a distraction-free zone to accomplish my goal.

Step 3: Manage Your Health

The process of developing a greater version of yourself requires good health. You can have talent, but without good health, you may not be able to develop the skill you need to increase your earning power in the marketplace. Some people are neglect their health – your health is your most valuable asset! Without it, you have nothing. Good health will generate more energy in your life to fulfill your vision.

Healthier people are more efficient and productive. When you are living with health issues, you have concerns and don't have peace of mind. This is especially true if you have a chronic disease. It can be very stressful to deal with. The bottom line is, you need to practice good health habits. I was not always good at managing my health.

At one time, I weighed about two hundred pounds. Based on my height and body mass, I was overweight. A lady I know but had not seen me for a period of time walked into my office, and before she even greeted me, she yelled, "Oh my gosh Pierre, you are getting too fat!" I had a few clients waiting for my services at that time and it was too embarrassing to even respond to her comment. But in reality, she was telling the truth. I weighed quite a bit more than I should have.

I took personal responsibility to self-correct this. I hired a coach from one of the local fitness centers and followed a regimen of regular exercise and a low-fat diet. Within six months, I brought my weight down to one hundred and seventy pounds and I've kept it down since then. Within a few months of working on my health, I went for a routine physical and my blood test showed signs of Type II diabetes.

I am convinced that if it was not for that lady's brutally honest criticism of my weight, I would not have made the changes that I did. My blood sugar level would be a lot worse and would be harder to control. God saw the direction that my health was going and He sent me a message to make changes. How could I fulfill my vision with bad health?

Step 4: Manage Your Energy

"What is a man without energy?
Nothing — nothing at all..."
— Mark Twain.

Developing a greater version of yourself requires both physical and mental energy; you don't have an unlimited supply of energy every day. Your energy is like the battery in your electronic device. It gets depleted, daily. However, in the same process that you can recharge your battery by connecting it to a power source, you can recharge and replenish your own energy with proper rest.

Not all of us have the same level of energy. Some people can work all day and still have plenty of energy left at the end of the day. Some people have more energy in the morning, but others are at their best in the evening. It is important to know when your energy is at its optimal level; it is best to perform your most important tasks during that time.

For example, I discovered that my energy is at its peak in the morning. Therefore, I try to accomplish my most important tasks and make my most important decisions in the morning. Even during my time in college, I tried to avoid taking classes in the evening because my energy level is not at its best in the evening.

Regardless of how important a task or a decision is, at the end of the day, if I don't have sufficient energy to get it done, it will not get done. I discipline myself to go to bed early unless I have a valid reason to stay up late. I get up very early in the morning to get an early start on my projects.

By three o'clock in the afternoon, I don't like to make any more decisions or start any new, important projects. This rhythm works for me.

Physical Energy

Your physical energy relates to your ability to perform physical activities; it relates to your physical strength and endurance. Your physical energy must not be taken for granted. If you are weak, your ability to perform both physically and mentally is reduced. Your ability to sit in one place for three to four hours and focus on accomplishing certain tasks is greatly dependent on your physical energy and strength.

Unfortunately, some people who are very goal-oriented tend to neglect themselves physically. They eat poorly and don't schedule time for daily physical exercise. While it should be your ambition to be goal-oriented and be successful in your journey, it is not wise to neglect your health in the process. It does not matter how much ambition you have, you will not reach your destination if your health is poor.

When I first started my career in real estate, I didn't take good care of myself. During the first five years I neglected to exercise and I didn't rest or eat well. I was constantly working long hours and eating at my desk. As a result, I put on an extra thirty pounds. Although I avoided eating greasy and fried food, my habits were still not healthy.

The types of food I was eating, including pasta and bread, were loaded with carbohydrates and fat. I didn't plan and take time to eat. I would grab something on the go when I felt hungry to the point of starvation, especially, when I didn't eat breakfast in the morning.

Research shows that when people don't eat breakfast, their bodies tend to store more fat, which increases their waistline. That was probably the cause of my thirty-pound weight surplus. I could have lost my health because my habits were not sustainable.

I will always be grateful for that lady's honesty to tell me the truth about my weight. It took that experience to motivate me to change my habits. Sometimes we need people who are not afraid to tell us the truth. The point is to pay attention to what you eat. Know what types of food to avoid and what types of food to eat. Good, nutritional food is not only good for energy, it is also good to reduce the risk of certain diseases, such as diabetes, high cholesterol, and high blood pressure. And also, don't forget to exercise in a regular basis!

Your Mental Energy

"The energy of the mind is the essence of life"
– Aristotle

Your mental energy relates your ability to focus, to concentrate, and to be alert. Your mind is very powerful and important in terms of your ability to think, to imagine, and to process information. In light of its importance, your mind needs to be plugged in and fully charged during your work or study performance hours. When your mind is fully charged you think better, and you can solve problems quicker and more effectively.

Step 5: Manage Your Self-Image

The ruler you use to measure your love for yourself is the same ruler you will apply to measure your love for others. You cannot give more love than you have. According to Jesus, there is no greater commandment than loving the Lord, your God, with all of your heart; all of your mind, and all of your strength, and loving your neighbor as yourself.

People who mistreat and criticize themselves are very dangerous to be around because they may not have enough love to share with you. If you are going to associate with them, you need to be aware.

Some people don't like themselves because of their physical appearance, or because they feel that they are not smart enough. My view about physical appearance is that it is not very important. Your physical appearance does not stay the same, it changes as you grow older. I believe your personal character is more important because it lasts to the end.

Having said that, if there is something you don't like about your physical appearance, then change it if you can. If you cannot change it, you must accept it as a fact, and move on. Believe me, how you look is not as important as who you are.

By the time I was about forty years old, I had started to lose the hair in the middle of my head and the forehead line was getting thinner. I didn't like it. I saw an ad about hair transplants and thought I should try it. Between the surgery, the treatments, and all the scheduled visits at the studio, I spent a lot of money and it still did not work for me.

In fact, I developed an allergic reaction to the products, and I got bumps all over my head. It was very painful to get rid of the bumps. Finally, I became completely bald, and now I look great. An expensive lesson!

Good self-image is about accepting yourself for who you are. People who do not accept themselves have more difficulty accepting others, and that causes many relationship problems. In particular, some people cannot keep a job long enough to complete the probationary period because their self-image is so poor that they cannot get along with anybody.

If anyone disagrees with their point of view, they get upset and become angry rather than talking through the issue. Sufficient self-confidence would allow them to deal with people who disagree with them.

Another problem some people have that affects their self-image is that they don't think they are smart enough. I believe everyone is smart in his or her own way. Just because someone is not an attorney, or does not have an MBA, does not say anything about the person's intelligence.

In your journey to success, you will meet many obstacles. A good self-image is what will keep you in the daily fight. The problem for some people is that their self-image is already weak. It is harder for them to fight, but self-image is much like your muscles. They may be weak, but if you determine to engage in exercise, you can build your muscles. Similarly, you can make a conscious decision to build your self-image.

Accepting Criticism Can Improve Yourself-Self-Image

Nobody likes criticism because it does not make us feel good about ourselves. The way to handle criticism is to remember that you are not perfect. As a result, others will see flaws, and find negative things to say about you. Rather than automatically dismiss criticism, let's consider that sometimes, it can be used to our benefit.

When others point out your flaws, if they are speaking the truth, you would do well to accept the criticism and take the necessary steps to fix the problem. One of the reasons that some people do not grow and make progress is that they don't like to hear the truth about themselves. As a result, they don't have the opportunity to correct their flaws and mistakes.

When you fix that flaw and correct your mistakes, you grow and change in a positive way. You become proud of yourself, and your self-image has the ability to be improved.

Although it is better to focus on our strengths instead of our weaknesses, mistakes need to be corrected so that we may learn and grow from them. It takes the grace of a healthy self-esteem to turn criticism into a learning opportunity.

The next time someone offers you a criticism, before you start taking it negatively and get your feelings hurt, take a good look at that criticism. Is it true? If it is true, there is only one thing to do – take the course of correction! You will be proud of yourself and it may improve your self-image. Having said that, I am also aware that some people will criticize you just to bring you down. In that instance, you need to find a way to keep your head up and not let them take you down.

Step 6: Manage Your Thoughts

Thoughts are creative and powerful. Your subconscious responds directly according to the direction of your thoughts. "As a man thinks in his heart, so is he," (Proverbs 23:7 NKJV). Everything you have or have not accomplished so far are the results of your prior thought process, and what you will achieve next year will be the direct response of your thought process this year.

If you think in terms of wealth, you can direct your thoughts toward developing a greater version of yourself to increase your earning power in the marketplace. If you think in terms of poverty and lack, you will think riches and wealth are not in your future.

If you don't like the result you are getting now, it is as simple as changing your thought pattern and focus your thoughts in the direction of the result you want. Your thoughts don't have any problem working for you and being your servants, but if you allow them, they will gladly be your masters.

Everything around us started with an idea in the mind of someone else. Have you ever thought about everything you see around you? The beautiful design of architecture, beautiful paintings, the nice automobile you love to drive, and the airplane that can take you to another country within hours – they were all thoughts and ideas in the minds of their inventors. Many of us who are seemingly poor are walking around with million-dollar ideas in our heads; we are just not ready to sign our names on the back of the check to cash it.

Are you ready to endorse your check? Some people underestimate the power of their thoughts. The power of your thoughts is far greater than your educational background, your history and your circumstances. It is all about the level of your thought vibration.

Positive people think at high-level vibrations; they think positive, healthy and empowering thoughts. However, negative people think at low-level vibrations. They think negative and disempowering thoughts. People who want to achieve great success need to operate at a higher level of thinking.

Many people have dreams but they don't act on them because they don't see how they can fulfill them. When a farmer plants a seed, he has no idea how the seed will sprout from the soil, his only job is to plant the seed. It is nature's job to make the seed sprout, grow, and produce fruit.

Some people never harvest any fruit because they never plant the seeds. Your mind cannot get to work to fulfill your vision until you plant the seed of your vision. Your mind is like fertile soil. It will grow whatever you plant in it, so you need to plant the seed of the fruit you want. For the same reason farmers clean soil before they plant their seeds, you also need to clean your heart before you plant your vision.

A seed cannot grow in contaminated soil. Your mind cannot give the result you want if your heart is contaminated with jealousy, hatred, anger, and resentment. You have to forgive people, clear your mind and heart, and move on in order to focus on your goals. You cannot carry all the baggage of your past and expect to succeed. Don't hold grudges.

Automatically forgive people and move on. I know this is easier to say than do. Seek help from your creator if you cannot do it naturally, but do it you must. I heard someone say, "If you put someone in jail, you need to watch him. You cannot be free while you are watching your prisoner."

To be free, you need to first set your prisoner free. Take no loss or offense with you. If you make a mistake, acknowledge it, learn the lesson, forgive yourself, and move on. Dwelling on your mistakes won't do you any good and will keep you from moving forward. To get the result you are after, you need a clear mind and clean conscience. If your thought process is defective, you cannot get accurate results.

You can nourish and water your ideas by reading inspirational books, listening to uplifting speeches, and with meditation and prayer. If you plant the seeds of success, they will grow success. If you plant the seeds of failure, they will grow failure. Simply by using his or her own thinking, a person can improve themselves, remain the same, or become worse.

"She can speak good or evil according to her thinking… for the mouth speaks what the heart is full of," (Luke 6:45 NIV). A man can decide to be a productive member of society and work to buy food and build shelter, or he can decide to beg for his food and sleep under bridges.

A man is not necessarily poor because of his environment or disabilities. Society is full of people with extreme disabilities who are making millions of dollars. A man is poor or rich based on his thinking. A person can bring themselves out of poverty by applying the right self-empowering thought process. A person is not necessarily limited by resources or lack of opportunities; they are only limited only by his or her imagination.

"Finally, brothers and sisters, whatever is true, whatever is noble, whatever is right, whatever is pure, whatever is lovely, whatever is admirable—if anything is excellent or praiseworthy—think about such things," (Philippians 4:8 NIV).

People who want to be successful need to learn how to master their thoughts and control their environment. "Above all else, guard your heart, for everything you do flows from it," (Proverbs 4:23 NIV). You need to train your mind to think right. It is like a fertile soil. Whatever you plant and nourish in your mind will grow and produce fruit, but it may not be the fruit you want.

Our mind is very complex, sophisticated, and powerful. It is one of the greatest assets each human being has. Scientists say that we are capable of receiving millions of bytes of information simultaneously via our five senses. Some research shows that we, as human beings, can originate about sixty thousand thoughts per day and our brain is capable of coordinating many activities simultaneously.

All thinking processes take place in our conscious mind. The conscious mind receives information through our five senses and analyzes the information before submitting this data to the subconscious mind. Once the information is submitted, the subconscious mind keeps it until it needs to act on it. The subconscious mind is like a memory bank. Whatever information it stores, it keeps permanently, and it can retrieve that information automatically, exactly as it was stored.

It is like a programmed computer. It responds exactly to whatever command it receives. The subconscious mind does not think or argue. It does not care about the quality of information being submitted, whether it be true or false; it will accept it "as is." Any judgment of the quality of the information has to be made at the conscious level. People who have been exposed to false information will constantly operate in error because their subconscious mind will spit out *exactly* what was stored.

To borrow from the colloquial, "garbage in, garbage out"; everything you are doing now is the product of past programming of your subconscious mind by the environment. People who want to be successful in life need to learn how to master their thoughts and control their environment.

Step 7: Manage Your Emotions

Emotional Intelligence (EI): Ability to regulate your own emotions, understand and deal with other people. EI is the newest marketing skill that experts in this field have been teaching for the past ten years. We have been taught to honor and admire people with high Intelligence Quotient (IQ), but recently, experts have discovered that EI is more important than IQ in succeeding in life.

The EI Principle has been with us for over two thousand years, we simply never applied it.

A priest accused a woman named Hannah of being a drunkard. "Not so, my Lord," Hannah replied, "I am a woman who is deeply troubled. I have not been drinking wine or beer; I was pouring out my soul to the Lord. Do not take your servant for a wicked woman; I have been praying here out of my great anguish and grief," (1 Samuel 15-16 NIV).

Eli answered, "Go in peace, and may the God of Israel grant you what you have asked of him," (1 Samuel 17 NIV).

Instead of letting the insult get to her, Hannah replied in a way to redirect the conversation and she recruited the Priest as her ally in prayer. In the Book of Matthew, we found another woman with high EI. The woman came and knelt before Jesus, "Lord, help me!" she said. Jesus replied, "It is not right to take the children's bread and toss it to the dogs."

"Yes, it is, Lord," she said. "Even the dogs eat the crumbs that fall from their master's table," (Matthew 15:25-27 NIV). People with high EI understand that it doesn't matter what happens or what others say. What matters are your interpretation and response.

Self-Awareness: According to an article in Harvard Business Review, January 4, 2018, by Tasha Eurich, self-awareness is how you see yourself and how other people see you.

Internal Self-Awareness: Is how you see yourself. Examine your values and passions. Know your strengths and weaknesses; your thoughts, feelings, and behaviors; why do you do the things you do?

External Self-Awareness: How do other people see you? "If there is any one secret of success, it lies in the ability to get the other person's point of view and see things from their angle, as well as your own," (Henry Ford). Most conflicts arise when we fail to see things from the other person's viewpoint.

It is not as simple as knowing yourself and how you are viewed by others, you have to balance both.

In the Office of an Immigration Officer, Elderly Woman Applying for Citizenship

I was in the immigration office with an elderly woman who was applying for her citizenship. I don't practice immigration law, but I was doing this as a favor for someone. Since the elderly woman was in a wheelchair, her daughter was there to assist. As we entered the room, the daughter asked me a question. I don't even recall the question, as it had nothing to do with the proceeding, but I made a mistake and answered in creole.

The officer was so offended, he took ten minutes or so to not only insult me, but the entire Haitian nation and immigrants in general. I could understand his feelings about the fact that I said something he didn't understand. I politely apologized to him and translated that one-word exchange between me and the interpreter from Creole to English.

But he wasn't satisfied. It was clear to me that his concern wasn't about the fact that I had spoken in Creole. He had other things he wanted to vent about immigrants and Haitians in particular, and he had been waiting for an opportunity.

I got very close to packing my things, leaving his office, and asking for his superior, but I thought about that elderly woman who wanted citizenship status. I remained quiet and let him vent. He looked at me like it was my turn to respond; like he was waiting to debate with me. Like, "I *dare* you to prove me wrong about anything I said about immigrants," but I stayed calm and very quiet. When he realized I wasn't going to respond, he collected his thoughts and proceeded with the interview.

Within the next five minutes, if you had not been in the room, you would not have known that just moments before, he was the same person spouting these negative things about immigrants and Haitians. Finally, he went above and beyond to make the process as smooth and easy as possible.

I believe I won him over by not engaging with his negativity. I tried to understand his frustration about the entire immigration and citizenship issues and let him vent. You can be very talented, and with a high IQ, but if you don't know how to interpret and respond to what others do and say, it will be difficult to succeed. When you set your goal to go after what you want, there will be outside influences to distract you from your original goal, but you have to remain focus on your original thoughts and desires.

Step 8: Manage Your Relationships

Some people can't make it far in life because they are good at burning their bridges. One of the most important things to understand is that society functions with people. You need help from people to succeed. You cannot succeed alone, no matter how intelligent and talented you are.

The smarter you are, the better you should know that you need a few allies you can count on. You need the help of your family, friends, and others. You need to learn how to build trust and credibility in any relationship; if you cannot be trusted, it is only a matter of time before all doors are closed to you. But if you can build and develop trust and credibility among your friends and peers, you will be in a stronger position to achieve your goals.

Things get easier when people trust you, but you will have a harder time making headway if you don't have credibility. I have seen people who acted without regard and consideration in their dealing with others. Be careful! You never know who might be in the position to give the help you need one day.

CHAPTER FIVE

Principle #5: The Power of Faith

"Without faith, no one can please God. Anyone who comes to God must believe that he is real and that he rewards those who truly want to find him."
(Hebrews 11:6)

What is faith?

Faith is your mental vision of your expected outcome. Realize that I said mental vision, not *physical* vision, because faith is not what you see with your physical eyes. Faith is what you see with your mental vision.

You have the confidence to take action toward achieving your goal because you *expect* a positive outcome. Any farmer can testify to that when he throws his seeds in the soil – he expects that they will come back and multiply. A few things happen with a seed: (1) First, you need to plant it. A seed does not become a tree until you plant it, and it can't produce fruit until it becomes a tree; (2) Second, you need to plant it in the right environment. Just leaving a seed on the cement floor does not do any good.

You need to do some work such as prepare the soil, dig a hole to put the seed in, and cover it with soil, and provide water and fertilization. Your mind is the soil in which your ideas and vision grow and produces success.

Faith cannot be passive. It has to be an action. The farmers take the leap of faith and plant their seeds knowing the universe will do its part to make the seeds sprout, grow and produce fruits. Similarly, your *ideas* are seeds. You need to exercise the faith of the farmers and plant your seeds with the expectation that they will and produce. Some people don't have enough self-confidence in their ideas and visions because their faith is weak. If you have weak faith, your self-confidence is also low. You will have the self-confidence to move forward with your project if you have enough faith to start.

Some people are very timid about their vision, to the point where they don't even want to talk about it. It is good to claim a clear vision and speak positively about it. You have to believe in it and have self-confidence that you *can* fulfill your vision. You need faith to succeed in life. Without it, you are not making it far.

Any successful person will tell you that you need faith to succeed. No person can ever achieve greatness without faith, no matter how talented and smart the person is. Watering will be rough and bad times will come. You need faith to navigate through the process of achieving your goals. No one can please God without faith.

How much faith do we need? Apparently not much. Jesus said, "if you have faith as small as a mustard seed, you can say to this mountain, 'Move from here to there,' and it will move. Nothing will be impossible for you," (Matthew

17:20 NIV). The Bible also teaches us, "It is given unto us as we believe."

I suspect that it is not the quantity of faith that is important. It is, rather, the *quality* of faith that matters. In other words, it is what you can see with your mind and believe. Apostle Paul said, "We walk by faith not by sight," (2 Corinthians 5:7).

There are so many challenges in life that living by sight can be very problematic. You will always see an obstacle you cannot overcome if you are operating by sight alone. Only when you are operating by faith, you won't get distracted by obstacles and problems.

My Greatest Discovery

We talk so much about the scientific discoveries that we have been making and how we can continue to alter our environment to better our lives. My greatest discovery is when I realized that there is a God in the universe, and He is living within every person, regardless of skin color, the nation of origin, or whether they are rich or poor. That infinite intelligence that I call God, His power, knowledge, and wisdom have no boundaries.

Every need and circumstance that we can ever face, the infinite intelligence living within us has the answer. Many of us are living unwanted lives of poverty and sickness simply because we don't know how to transform ourselves. No matter what your circumstances are today, you can lead yourself out by tapping into that source of power within you. Jesus said, "I came so they can have real and eternal life, a better life than they ever dreamed of," (John 10:10 MSG).

I also came to learn that there is no lack in the universe. Scarcity is an economic concept. That concept does not exist in God's economy. The resources in the universe are not limited. You are limited only to the extent of your faith. "Let it be done to you according to your faith," (Matthew 9: 29).

We can never finish harvesting all the resources of the universe. The entire $317 trillion of the Global Wealth and growing will never leave this planet. "God gives us richly, all things to enjoy," (1 Timothy 6: 17). Coming from an environment where everything seems to be limited, the above discoveries have been very significant to me, and I suspect they are important to you as well.

CHAPTER SIX

Principle #6: Giving Back, Saving and Investing

In the previous chapter, we mentioned that one's natural talent will become the source of their wealth. You can earn income by developing your talents, inventing something, improving a product, or by providing a valuable service in the marketplace. Your talent is like your golden chicken laying golden eggs to make you rich.

But you cannot eat or give away all the eggs your golden chicken has produced. You have to allow some of your eggs to hatch in order for them to reproduce more of their kind to increase your egg production. In other words, you cannot spend every dollar that your talent produces for you. You have to save a percentage of that income to reproduce more of its kind.

10/10/80 Principle

The 10/10/80 Principle is easy to explain. It says that for every ten dollars your talent earns you, you give $1.00 to your favorite charity. Next, you pay yourself (your savings) $1.00 and you keep $8.00 to spend. $8.00 is all you have to spend, but you can spend it any way you want as long as you respect the principle.

Some people may not like to follow rules but let me remind you that we are living in a law-governed universe set by the Creator. For example, we have the Law of Gravity. We can disobey it if we want, but it may be at our own peril. Every government's citizens must obey the laws for a good and orderly governance of the society. Similarly, there are rules to follow in order to be financially prosperous.

Give Back the First Ten Percent to Your Favorite Charity

You give back to the society the first ten percent of what your talent earned you as a sign of gratitude to God for giving you the talent, physical strength and intelligence to earn money, as well as a sign of faith of continuance in your financial abundance. This is a Biblical Principle that has been practiced since the Old Testament.

People who have applied this testified that it brought financial miracles into their lives. God, Himself, guaranteed that if you follow this rule, you can never be poor. "I am the LORD All-Powerful, and I challenge you to put me to the test. Bring the entire ten percent into the storehouse, so there will be food in my house. Then I will open the windows of Heaven and flood you with blessing after blessing," (Malachi 3:10). Jesus also taught the Principle of Giving and Receiving. He said: "The measure you give will be the measure you get," (Luke 6:38).

Pay Yourself A Percentage of Each Dollar That Your Talent Earns

The way some financial advisors put it is that we all earn money just to pay bills. It is true because none of us are taking money with us when we leave this planet. Every dollar we make will stay here to pay bills, either by us or our loved ones, who stay behind. Since you are the General Manager of your talent, why don't you try paying yourself a percentage of what your talent has earned you? The most popular percentage is 10%.

For every ten dollars that your talent brings you, you pay yourself one dollar. You don't spend that dollar. You keep it in a savings account or another investment to reproduce more of its own kind. It is easy and simple. Most of the principles of success are easy and simple – the most difficult part is starting, but once you start applying them, they become second nature.

The purpose of keeping this dollar saved is to insure a future income for you. We all will come to an age when we lose the physical and mental capacity to produce and generate income. This is a fact of life. All of us will get to this point in our lives unless we die prematurely.

It is your responsibility to make a plan for that day when you can no longer produce or use your talents as you once could. This is not a trivial matter. People are living much longer now with chronic diseases. As a result, the cost to keep you alive is more, and you cannot expect society to take care of that cost. You will live in pain and suffering if you don't make a long-term plan.

Eighty Percent for You to Spend as You Please

For some people, the challenge may be that the entirety of what they earn is not enough to make ends meet. How can they afford to give 10% away and save another 10%? First of all, you have to make a distinction between what you may call necessary expenses and what you may desire because of your sophisticated taste.

For example, I may need transportation, but I don't need a Maserati. A Maserati is what my tastes may desire, but it is not a necessary expense. Now, there is nothing wrong taking pleasure in and enjoying driving my Maserati as long as I pay for it out of 80% of what my talent has earned me, which was mine to spend as I please. However, even when I can pay for it out of my 80%, I have to be careful.

Just because I am making more doesn't mean I have to keep feeding my monster taste. I have to have restraint because my desire for stuff can easily exceed my earnings. The spending habit is a monster with a hungry taste for more stuff we don't really need. If we don't restrain it, it will eat all our earnings because it will always be hungry for more.

I also know that there are fixed expenses such as, shelter, food, and health care, which you don't have any control over. It is possible that these costs can exceed your earnings. If you are truly not earning enough to meet your necessary needs, which happens commonly, the solution for this is to go back and reread the chapter on developing a greater version of yourself to increase your ability to earn more.

Learn How to Invest the Dollar You Pay Yourself

The dollar you keep and save is a start, but it does not mean much if it is not producing more of its own kind. In fact, the dollar you save today will decrease in value tomorrow because of inflation. Turn your saving's dollars into an army to protect your financial future by reinvesting them back into the marketplace.

At some point, your dollar should be working for you instead of you working for your dollar. The harder your dollar can work for you, the faster you can become wealthy. Many people think that they are wealthy because of the amount money they have in the bank, but it is not so. The value of your wealth is not measured by the size of your bank account, but rather, by its ability to produce more of its own kind. You don't get rich by keeping the dollar in a safe. You have to make it multiply.

Get the Advice of Good Professional Financial Advisors

Investment can be very tricky. It requires the advice of scrupulous professional financial advisors if you don't know what you are doing. I know many people who have lost their life savings because some unscrupulous people posed as financial advisors and took advantage of them.

Stay away from people who promise to double your money overnight. It is *not* true. There is a saying: "if it's too good to be true, it may not be true". This is good advice to keep in mind. When looking for a professional advisor, be sure to check out qualifications, experience, integrities, and please don't take financial advice from your barber, your hairdresser, or auto mechanic, either. It does not matter how long you know them, even if they are good and honest people who have your best interest at heart; they just don't qualify to give you financial advice.

If they know a good financial advisor they dealt with in the past and they are satisfied with the service, they can refer you, but you still have to do your own investigating. Before you start investing, you also need to establish your goal for the money you are investing.

For example, are you investing to raise enough for a down payment to buy your first home or are you investing for your retirement? Clarifying that goal will help to determine whether you will make a long-term or short-term investment.

Real Estate Investment

If you haven't found a better investment's vehicle, to invest your money, you should definitely consider real estate.

Homeownership is the first step toward financial stability because investing in your first home can be a source of financial security. I purchased my first home using a Federal Housing Administration (FHA) loan. FHA is a governmental program that insures loans for individuals who cannot come up with a 20% down payment to qualify for a loan.

Under this program, people can make their first investment in real estate with as little as a 3.5 percent down payment. In my case, I used up my entire five-thousand-dollar savings to make my first real estate investment. Within two years, I already purchased a second home to occupy as my primary residence and rented the first one as income producing property. Within three years later, I sold the first property and walked away with thirty thousand dollars and started my real estate brokerage business. As a Real Estate Broker with more than two decades of experience, I helped hundreds of clients start their first real estate investments applying the same principles.

I disagree with the investors who are teaching that a homestead property is a liability, not an asset.

What other investment could give this kind of above return on my five thousand dollars, plus, get me started on my career as a real estate investor? It is not a guarantee that everyone will make the same positive return. Real estate can increase and decrease in value. You just have to get in it with a long-term perspective.

According to the historical housing price data from the National Association of Realtors (NAR), median home prices in the 60s were around twenty-thousand dollars. In 2019, the average home prices were two-hundred and fifty-six-thousand dollars.

There may be a reason why you cannot make your first real estate investment right now, but whatever the reason is, renting cannot be your long-term strategy. The sooner you make your first purchase, the sooner you can start building equity.

CHAPTER SEVEN

Principle #7:
Now You've Earned it,
Protect it

The main purpose of this book is to challenge you to develop a greater version of yourself to increase your earning power and build enough assets to create financial security and peace of mind against financial burden. Unfortunately, we are living in a very litigious society.

Individuals and businesses are getting sued every day. The need to legally protect what you have worked so hard to build has never been greater. As a lawyer, it wouldn't be a credit to you if I didn't take the time to warn you about the risk of not protecting what you've built.

First, you need to protect your wealth against unscrupulous investors who have the potential to cause you to lose your money overnight. Once you start building some assets, there will be many people posing as expert financial advisors who will promise to grow your assets. Be fully aware that they may not be able to deliver what they are promising.

I have received too many phone calls from people who are being victimized by so-called financial advisors. The people who are least educated are the most vulnerable to predators. Secondly, you need to protect your assets against other people who may want to sue just because they think you may have money, and to them, the easiest way to get what you have is by some sort of frivolous lawsuit.

What is Asset Protection?

Asset protection is a set of legal strategies to shield what you have worked so hard to earn against lawsuits by creditors or any other litigants who may want to take it from you. There are people who are sniffing around and looking for other people with unprotected assets to sue for. If your assets are not protected, you are open and exposed to this kind of fraudulent behavior.

What's even worse, is that there are lawyers who are encouraging people to look for their next victims. As a lawyer myself, I am not against lawsuits. If someone is injured, he or she must be compensated. What I am completely against is the fabrication of the lawsuits. This is a very litigious society, in that anybody can get sued. You can get sued for the act of your partner, your associate, or even for the act of your child.

Anyone with a car driving on the road can get sued. We are all at risk. The only one thing you can do is minimize your risk of exposure and legally shield your assets against lawsuits. We used to think that people couldn't file frivolous lawsuits, but now, even the most frivolous lawsuits are making their way in court.

Some lawyers filed these lawsuits without any expectation of winning on their merit, but with the hope that they can intimidate their victims into settlement just to make the suits go away. These types of lawsuits are extortions and they shouldn't be allowed in the courtrooms. In this litigious environment, you have an obligation to protect what you have.

How Does Asset Protection Work?

Each state has different laws for asset protection. You will have to consult with a competent attorney where your assets are located for legal advice. The basic answer depends on what asset you want to protect and how soon you want the protection. For example, if you wait until you get sued to seek for asset protection, it might be too late. The best practice is to put the protection in place at the time you acquire the asset, or as soon as you are able to do so.

Insurance

You cannot totally avoid risk, but you can manage it. Insurance allows you to manage the risk by shifting it to an insurance company. You pay a premium to an insurance company to assume the risks associated with your real estate property, your automobile, your health, and even your life; this is your first line of defense in asset protection. You should always have sufficient insurance coverage at all times.

Inside and Outside Risks of Your Asset

Making plans to protect your asset requires a good understanding of where the threats are coming from so that you can have the appropriate protection for each threat. Typically, your asset can be exposed to both inside and outside risks.

Inside Risk

Inside risk is where you can get sued in connection with a particular property you owned, or in connection with a service you are rendering as your profession. For example, if you own a rental property and someone is injured on that rental property because of your negligence or the negligence of your property manager, you can get sued individually as the property owner. If the injured person wins a judgment because of his or her injury, that judgment will be both against you, individually, and the rental property.

At that point, the judgment can be attached to any other asset you have in your name, including your personal bank account. The same can happen in your practice as a doctor, a lawyer, or a hairdresser. If someone is injured as a result of a service you provided, both you and your business may be liable.

Outside Risk

Outside risk is the risk that is associated with you, personally. For example, anytime you get behind the wheel of a vehicle and take the public roads, you are exposed to risk. If you are at fault in an automobile accident and you cause injuries to someone else, everything you have in your personal name can be attached to the claim.

How to Shield Your Asset Against Potential Claims

There are many Federal and state laws for protection of some of your personal assets, such as: (1) Homestead exemption laws (2); your individual retirement account (IRA); (3) your annuity plan; (4) your life insurance policy; (5) your social security benefits, and (6) properties held by the entireties. The above assets are exempt from creditor's claims.

Corporation, Limited Liability Company (LLC) or Limited Partnership (LP)

The above entities can protect against insider threats. For example, if instead of holding the title of your rental property on your name, you hold the title under an LLC, any judgment for a claim associated with the rental property will be against only the LLC that owned the rental property. That judgment will not be against any other asset on your personal name unless you are individually participating in the misconduct that caused the claim.

Entities Are Not Exempt from Claims

Corporations, LLCs and LPs are not exempt from claims. A creditor can still sue your LLC and get a charging order. A charging order will allow a creditor to satisfy its claim from the percentage of your interest in the LLC. They provide protection only against forced sales or foreclosure of your properties.

If there is a judgment against you as a member of an LLC, that judgment is limited only to a charging order. In addition, even with that piece of paper, "charging order", the creditor cannot force a corporation or multiple members of an LLC to make a distribution to the member of the LLC the creditor has the charging order against.

The judgment holder can only wait for when or if a distribution is made to the member and then grab it. In some jurisdictions, a judgment creditor who is tired of waiting may petition a court to foreclose on the debtor's percentage of interest (a debtor is the individual or the entity the claim of judgment is against).

Florida does not allow such a foreclosure proceeding, at least not yet. However, to get the benefits of the above protection, the LLC must be properly run and administrated. Again, people seeking for asset protection must consult a competent attorney in the jurisdiction where the property is located to make sure that proper protection is in place and well administrated.

Corporation is Not a Good Choice for Asset Protection

Unlike Limited Partnership (LP) and Multiple Members Limited Liability Company (LLC), a corporation is not a good choice for asset protection. As previously discussed, if you hold your assets under an LLC or LP, a judgment holder creditor's right is limited only to a charging order.

However, a judgment holder creditor can foreclose on the interest of a corporation's shareholder who is subject to a judgment, and the judgment holder creditor can take complete control of the debtor's share. If the judgment holder creditor becomes a controlling shareholder, that can further complicate the operation of the corporation.

Protecting Your Liquidated Estate Asset

Some people hold their savings, checking accounts, CDs, mutual funds, and bonds under their personal names. Unless these assets are exempt by federal and state exemption laws, they are exposed to high risk. A judgment holder creditor can freeze and take over these assets from your financial institutions.

In most cases, you can hold these as tenancy by the entireties, and that will provide enough protection, but in a case where there is a large sum of liquidated assets, it might be better to hold these assets in a Limited Partnership (LP). Again, it is very important to consult with a competent attorney before you decide. I don't encourage the do-it-yourself approach!

CHAPTER EIGHT

Principle #8: The Proper Distribution of Your Assets

No one ever left this planet with the assets that he or she created, and you won't either. Everything you have created will stay here to help those you will leave behind. The real enjoyment in being rich is not when you spend what you have selfishly on yourself, the real enjoyment is when you help the least fortunate and make a difference in the lives of others.

With that in mind, you have to create a system of a proper distribution of your assets. Every honorable person thinks about a proper division of assets before God calls him home.

Your Estate

After you die, the assets you leave behind are called your estate. It is everything you own at the time of your death, including your real estate, bank accounts, retirement savings, and life insurance.

Probate

If you die without leaving behind a system for proper distribution of your wealth, the state where you lived at the time of your death will make one up for you through a process called intestate succession. Intestate succession is a set of rules created by the state to determine who should receive the assets you had in your name at your time of death. For example, if you have a spouse and children, they are first in line.

If there is no spouse or children, your grandchildren, if any, will receive your assets, and that will be followed by your parents, brothers, sisters, nieces, and nephews, if any. The problem with this process is that the state may not distribute your assets according to your wish.

For example, you may wish to leave more for a child with a special need, or you may wish to leave a portion of assets to your favorite charity. Without any instructions to express your wishes, you leave it to the state to decide for you. Did you know that if you die without leaving any instructions on how your assets should be distributed, and if the state cannot locate any of your heirs, it will keep your entire estate?

A Written Will

A written will is one of the instructions you can leave behind on how you want your assets to distribute after you die. You can also give specific instructions about your funeral arrangements. The court will respect and follow your will unless someone challenges the will and the court has reason to believe that the will does not reflect your true intent. In that case, the will may not be admitted.

Trust

A trust is another legal document you can use to distribute your assets. Your assets are placed in the trust, and you or someone you trust will manage the assets during your lifetime. You or the person of your choice will be the trustee. The trust allows you to transfer the legal title of your assets to the trustee. If you name yourself as the trustee, you need to name another person as the successor trustee in case of your incapacity, or upon your death.

There are two types of trusts: Revocable and Irrevocable Trust. A revocable trust is a trust you can change, amend or revoke during your lifetime, but it becomes irrevocable upon your death. An irrevocable trust can't be changed.

Will vs. Trust, What's the Difference?

Both will and trust are legal documents giving instructions on how to distribute your assets upon death. The difference between these two legal documents is that the will still needs be probated. That means, a judge will have to validate the will before the assets can be distributed. The probate process is expensive and can take a long time before your assets are distributed.

With a trust, there is no need for probate. Upon your death, your trustee has the legal authority to distribute your assets immediately according to the Trust Agreement. Essentially, both will and trust have a similar purpose, except that trust allows you to avoid probate.

Joint Tenancy with Right of Survivorship

The assets you owned jointly with right of survivorship, such as assets you owned jointly with your spouse, do not require a probate. If one person dies, the title automatically transfers into the name of the other joint tenant.

Life Insurance, Bank and Retirement Accounts

With these assets, you can name your beneficiaries. Upon your death, all it requires is the death certificate. The benefits will be immediately paid to your beneficiaries.

The Executor of the Will

If you choose to create a will instead of a trust, you need to designate an executor. An executor is the person who submits the will to the court for approval. Upon approval of the will, the executor is officially approved by the court to conduct business in the name of the estate. The executor's job is very important.

Not only that, the executor is responsible for collecting all the assets of the estate, and he or she is responsible to seek and identify all debtors of the estate. Distribution cannot be made without the court approval and he or she needs to keep good records. The most dangerous aspect of the executor's job is that an executor can be sued and held personally liable for any mistakes or wrongful distribution of property.

CHAPTER NINE

What Do You Do Now?

"Knowledge has no value until it is applied."
– Pierre St-Jean

Congratulations! Now that you have read the Eight Proven Principles to Prosperity. In the previous chapters, you have taken a giant step towards the life you dream of and deserve. Not everyone can do this.

The next step is to take action. Knowledge is important, but it is of no value to you until you put it into action. After each question below, I intentionally leave space for you to write your answers, thoughts, and comments. If you wish to share them with me, I welcome that. I would love to keep the conversation going.

Make Yourself Valuable

1. In your line of profession, how valuable are you?

2. What can you do to become more valuable?

3. If you are self-employed, how valuable are you to your clients? Are you knowledgeable enough to solve your clients' problems efficiently?

4. Are you taking continuing education to stay up to date?

5. How many books are you reading every month related to your line of work to make yourself more valuable?

6. If you are working for a company, are you adding value, or are you just a cost to the company?

7. What problem or problems can you solve for the company to make it more profitable?

8. When people are looking for an expert in your field of work, are they looking for you? How do you know this?

9. Can you honestly solve their problems effectively and efficiently? "Be faithful in what you do now, and you will be master over bigger things. "

10. Determine what additional training or education you need to become more valuable in your field of work and commit yourself to get that additional training or education. For example, if you are in the medical field, what additional training do you need to reach the next level? If you are an electrician, plumber, or carpenter, you need to take the next step to be the general contractor.

11. When can you start?

Self-Discovery

1. Identify your desires, concerns, discontents, aspirations, ambitions, hopes, worries, and fears. For me, my fear was an inferiority complex, and that I might never be more than a farmworker because my education level was too low. Yours may be different, but identify it so you can face it.

2. Are you happy with your current financial condition?

3. If not, what needs to change? Remember, for things to change, you need to change.

4. Do you think you will have enough financial resources to support yourself when you can no longer work? Or are you relying on Social Security Income?

5. If you don't have a personal retirement plan, what can you do now?

6. Are you financially secure and have peace of mind against financial burdens?

7. If not, what can you do now?

8. What is the natural talent that you were born with?

9. Have you developed that talent into a skill to earn you income?

10. Are you getting pay for your talent or are you giving it away for free?

11. What is your personal vision? Write it down.

12. Now create goals and action steps to fulfill your vision.

13. Be clear, specific about your goals, and set a deadline to accomplish your goals.

14. Identify available resources around you and do what you can where you are with what you have.

Personal Responsibility

1. Do you agree that you are 100% in charge of your success?

2. If you agree, what are the steps are you willing to take now to establish financial security and peace of mind against financial burn?

3. Can you take the first step today? If not, can you at least commit to a specific date? For example, your first step maybe as simply as taking a trip to the local college, university, or the technical school to register for a class.

Self-Management

1. How do you manage your time?

2. Do you keep a priority journal to determine what tasks that will have greater positive impact on your vision?

Your Faith

1. What does faith mean to you?

2. Where is the source of your faith?

3. How does your faith serve you?

Giving Back / Saving / Investing – 10/10/80 Principle

1. How much do you give back to your favorite charitable organization?

2. How much do you save?

3. Do you have an investment portfolio that is giving positive return on your dollar? If not, when can you take the step to establish one?

4. Do you keep your taste for more stuff under control?

5. Do you have the courage to say no when your monster taste is asking for more stuff you don't need?

Protect what you have built

1. Are your assets protected?

2. If not, you need to take steep now. Don't wait until you get suite. It will be too late.

Proper distribution of your assets upon your death

1. Do you have clear written instructions how to distribute your assets after you die?

2. If not, do it today to help your love ones with the complicated legal proceeding call "Probate".

Live Life to Succeed!

Pierre St. Jean

Share These Books With Others

If you're working hard but getting nowhere financially, stand up and take control of your life! You are responsible for your success or failure. But when you're ready to break through every obstacle preventing you from accumulating wealth, Pierre St. Jean's proven principles will transform your relationship with money while also strengthening every other area of your life.

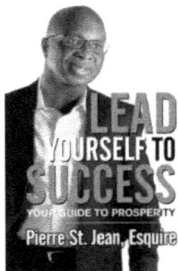

SPECIAL QUANTITY DISCOUNTS

2-20 Books .... $19.00 each
21 – 99 Books .... $16.50 each
100 – 299 Books .... $14.50 each
300 – 399 .... $10.00 each

In this book, you will read about some of the most powerful principles of success he has applied to lead himself from an immigrant farm worker to a lawyer and a successful businessman.

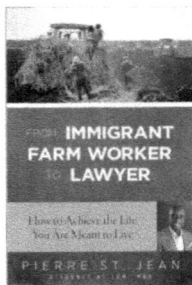

SPECIAL QUANTITY DISCOUNTS

2-20 Books .... $13.00 each
21 – 99 Books .... $11.50 each
100 – 299 Books .... $9.50 each
300 – 399 .... $7.50 each

To place an order, call 561-721-0022

Book Pierre St. Jean to Speak to Your Audience

Pierre St. Jean will hold your audience spellbound as he retells his story from an immigrant farmworker to a lawyer.

Destined to stay in generational poverty, Pierre determined to do whatever it took to rise above and succeed.

The lessons he learned along the way will inspire, empower and motivate your audience to take charge of their lives and lead themselves to success. No victim mentality allowed.

To book Pierre St. Jean to speak to your audience, email him at Pierre@pstjean.com

Or call him at 561-721-0022